TOURIST'S GUIDE

TO

CORNWALL

AND

THE SCILLY ISLES:

CONTAINING

SUCCINCT INFORMATION CONCERNING ALL THE PRINCIPAL PLACES AND OBJECTS OF INTEREST IN THE COUNTY.

BY

WALTER H. TREGELLAS,

CHIEF DRAUGHTSMAN, WAR OFFICE ;
MEMBER OF THE ROYAL ARCHÆOLOGICAL INSTITUTE OF GREAT BRITAIN
AND IRELAND,
AND CORRESPONDING MEMBER OF THE ROYAL INSTITUTION OF CORNWALL;
AUTHOR OF 'CHINA: THE COUNTRY, ITS HISTORY, AND PEOPLE,' &C., &C.

" Nescio quâ natale solum dulcedine cunctos
Ducit, et immemores non sinit esse sui."

With a Map.

LONDON:

EDWARD STANFORD, 55, CHARING CROSS, S.W.

—

1878.

TOURIST'S GUIDE

TO

CORNWALL

AND THE

SCILLY ISLES.

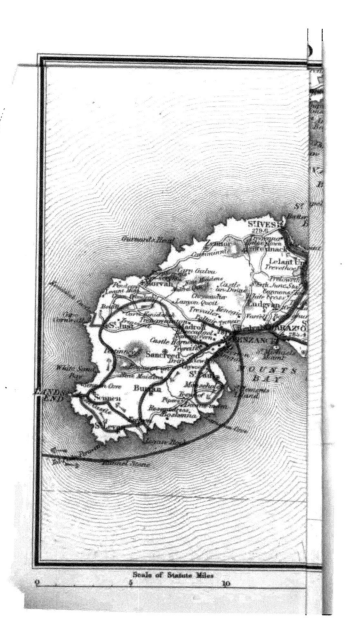

Scale of Statute Miles
0   5   10

PREFACE.

A few words by way of preface seem desirable in the case of this handbook, because it must necessarily differ in some respects from others of the series which Mr. Stanford is publishing.

In the first place, it does not profess to be a *Gazetteer* or *Directory* to the county of Cornwall, nor to give such minute descriptions as to render a visit almost unnecessary. This would, in all probability, have resulted in a mass of information about many places which possess comparatively little interest for the tourist, and which are, moreover, difficult of access.

Nor does it assume to give *exhaustive* descriptions of each of the numerous places of interest mentioned; to have given such would have swelled the volume to a size unsuitable for a knapsack. I have, however, endeavoured to deal pretty fully with all of those centres of interest which long experience indicates as the most attractive to visitors; and have, whenever it seemed desirable, given hints as to other sources of information to those who may be desirous of extending their researches.

Whenever it has been practicable, I have endeavoured to give the meaning of the Cornish names of places, in the belief that such would not only add to the intelligent interest of the stranger, but would often throw a light upon the history or situation of the place described—*conveniunt locis nomina sæpissime.* It should, however, be added that, owing to circumstances which will be referred to in their proper place, the etymology of Cornish names can seldom be discovered with certainty.

The introductory chapter comprises an unusual number of sections; but Cornwall has many interesting specialities, and I hope the reader will think that the subdivisions of the chapter are not too many to assist him in attaining a full and correct appreciation of the subject.

Few will be more conscious than the writer himself is of the imperfections of this little attempt to describe the main attractions of his native county; but, as he is "de la vieille roche," he trusts that his brother Cornishmen will, "one and all," assist him with their suggestions towards making a future edition more complete.

MORLAH LODGE, TREGUNTER ROAD,
    BROMPTON, S.W.,
        Christmas, 1877.

CONTENTS.

———◦◦———

ABBREVIATIONS.

R.I.C.J.—Journal of the Royal Institution of Cornwall.
[ ] indicate deviations from the main route.

TOURIST'S GUIDE

TO

CORNWALL AND THE SCILLY ISLES.

INTRODUCTORY CHAPTER.

PHYSICAL GEOGRAPHY AND GEOLOGY.

THE coast line of Cornwall — the southernmost and westernmost county of England (see map) — may, like that of Italy, be not inaptly compared to the shape of a Wellington boot, the iron heel of which is the mass of serpentine which forms the southern point of the Lizard district, and the foot that part which lies between Mount's Bay and Land's End. The instep is at St. Ives Bay; and the body of the boot constitutes the main portion of the county. The position of the calf has unfortunately got reversed, and instead of being where it *should* be—at St. Austell Bay—is to be found along that district of the *northern* shore lying between Tintagel and Newquay, with Padstow in the middle of the prominence. Falmouth harbour is the place for the spur, and the top of the boot is of course represented by the line of the Tamar. To complete the resemblance to the map of Italy, the football Sicily is represented, in the case of Cornwall, by the Scilly Isles; which, however, instead of lying close to the toe of the boot, are 25 miles S.W. of the Land's End.

A great ridge runs down the middle of the county, the highest bosses being towards the eastern end, and forming the Bodmin Moors. From this ridge the streams descend northwards to the Bristol Channel and southwards to the English—the rivers and bays on the southern side being by far the more numerous and considerable. Along the northern coast the lofty mural cliffs with their horizontal strata — "giant warders of the deep" — against which the Atlantic rollers for ever break in measured cadences

B

of thunder, offer a marked contrast to the perpendicular
stratification, and tamer but more sylvan scenery, which
surround the shores and harbours * of the south and
south-west.   When we add that, across the low-lying
lands between the St. Ives and the Mount's Bays, the
seas have threatened to meet at spring tides, enough
will probably have been said to give our readers a rough
notion of the physical configuration of the county; yet
our account would be incomplete without a passing
reference to the Legend of Lionnesse, narrated by Camden,
Whitaker, and others, from the accounts given by more
than one mediæval writer.   According to Florence of
Worcester, 140 parish churches were buried in the sea
between the Mount and Scilly.   When, however, we
consider, as Mr. Whitley has pointed out, that 140
average parishes would represent two-thirds of the area
of all Cornwall, and that the soundings between the
Land's End and Scilly are between 30 and 40 fathoms, it
seems only necessary to mention this time-honoured story
in order to consign it to oblivion.

As to the Geology of Cornwall, volumes † a hundred
times the bulk of this have been written, and ample
details may be found, by those who are deeply interested
in the subject, in the Transactions of the Royal Geological
Society of Cornwall, at Penzance.   The following brief
sketch will probably satisfy the requirements of the
ordinary tourist.   Generally speaking then, the oldest
or Cambrian rocks are on the S. coast.   Next in order
of antiquity, and constituting the bulk of the county, are
the Devon limestones and grits.   The N.E. district of
Cornwall, composed of carboniferous rocks, succeeds.
This portion consists, first, of a belt of mountain limestone
from 2 to 3 miles wide, which stretches across this corner
of the county for about 15 miles from Launceston to
Forrabury; and secondly, of the millstone grits, which complete our northernmost triangle.   Finally comes the back-
bone of the county, the four main granite masses, thrust up
north-eastward through strata perhaps previously weak-
ened by the action of fire.   The *first* of these granite
bosses covers an area of about 12 miles by 10, with

* The harbours of South Cornwall were of much importance
before the days of vessels of deep draft, and of railways.
  † Notably Sir Henry de la Beche's great work on the 'Geology
of Cornwall, Devon, and West Somerset,' 1837.

Dozmare Pool nearly in its centre ; the *second*, of about half the area, and the chief seat of the china clay and growan deposits, which lies between St. Stephens and Lostwithiel ; the *third*, which occupies the district lying between Camborne, Redruth, Penryn, and Helston, and from which the celebrated building granite of Constantine, which has been so extensively used in many important structures in London, at Chatham Docks, and on Plymouth Breakwater, is obtained ; and the *fourth*, which composes the western extremity of the county lying between St. Ives and Penzance, known as the Land's End District, and extends to the Scilly Isles. Here it is instructive to note how all the main valleys run parallel to each other in the direction of the great granite joints.

It will be of course understood that this is only a very rough outline of the subject ; but enough has probably been said to demonstrate that only the most ancient geological epochs, the *Palæozoic*, are represented in Cornwall.* Under such circumstances the rarity of fossils will not be wondered at. Some are found, e. g., *Spirifera disjuncta* in the slate rocks near Tintagel ; and others (chiefly Polypiaria) at Looe, Fowey, St. Columb, and Talland Bay ; but, with the exception of the specimens found in the narrow seams of mountain limestone known as the Petherwin group, fossils in Cornwall are few and far between. Lysons wrote, in 1814, that none had ever been found here. With a brief reference to the interesting phenomena of raised beaches and submerged forests, occasionally met with along the coast, this section of our remarks must conclude. Striking examples of the former may be inspected in the Land's End District, also between Falmouth and the Lizard, and near St. Ives ; of the latter at Looe, Mount's Bay, Hayle, St. Columb Porth, Padstow, and Perranzabuloe. The raised beaches, sometimes 40 or 50 feet above present high water-mark, of course indicate that there has been an elevation of the land, and the submerged forests a depression ; but it should be borne in mind that all are not " raised beaches " that at first

* The great *metalliferous* districts are mainly composed of the Devonian slates—especially the lowest of the series, the copper-bearing " *killas* " of Marazion, Camborne, Redruth, and Gwennap ; whilst the exquisitely beautiful serpentine, of igneous origin, is almost entirely confined to the district round the Lizard, and a small patch at Clicker Tor, near Liskeard.

sight appear so : indeed, some that have been too hastily
so termed are more probably old river beds ; nor do
submerged forests necessarily indicate a very remote
antiquity for their destruction.

As bearing on the peculiar configuration of Cornwall,
it may here be observed that more than one attempt has
been made to evade the circumnavigation of the Land's
End by constructing canals and other routes across the
county.* One such attempt was made in 1796 between
Wadebridge and Lostwithiel, under Act of Parliament,
37 Geo. III. ; but the great cost of a long tunnel, which
was found necessary, prevented the execution of the
project. The next step was a tramway between Falmouth harbour and Portreath ; and the problem was at
last satisfactorily solved by the late Mr. Treffry of
Fowey, who commenced, but did not complete the Cornwall Minerals Railway between Fowey and Newquay.
This has recently been acquired by the Great Western
Railway Company, and adapted for passenger traffic.

HISTORY.

It would not be practicable (even if it were desirable),
considering the limited space at our command, to enter
upon that vague field of learned discussion, the condition
of Cornwall before the Roman invasion ; the limits of the
Cimbri, the Carnabii, and the Damnonii ; or her ancient
Phœnician commerce.† It will probably suffice for our
purpose to note that, though the early history of the
county—the Cassiterides of the ancients—is obscured
by the mists of remotest ages, and, though even the
Druids are only vaguely mentioned by two or three of
the Latin writers, such as Cæsar and Pliny, yet there are
not wanting indications of the early greatness of her
trade in British times ; nor of the probability that, at the
period of the Roman invasions, Cornwall had already somewhat fallen from her former high estate.

The Roman occupation of Britain can, however, scarcely
be said to have penetrated Cornwall, though this county
nominally formed part of their Britannia Prima ; traces
of it are to be found in the names of a few places, imper-

---

* A similar scheme for connecting the English and Bristol
Channels was devised by Telford, who once projected a canal
between Bridgewater and Axmouth.
† Cf. Smith's ' Cassiterides.'

fectly identified, and in those characteristic roads, which, however, in Cornwall are for the most part on the lines of more ancient British tracks.* But in fact, at this period distant Cornwall was almost beneath Roman notice. Stray coins of some of the earlier emperors, and Brito-Roman inscribed stones, &c., have been found at sundry points, even in remote Penwith; but they are comparatively few and far between. With the age of the Antonines the proportion slightly increases, but it is not until the middle of the 3rd century that they appear in any considerable quantities; all denoting that no permanent Roman settlement of importance was made in the county. We need not, however, linger long over this part of the subject, but may at once proceed to the times of the English conquest.

The history of the Cornwall men—the Cornwealhas †— or "*foreigners* of the horn-shaped land" (for such the English considered and named them), now begins to be what the peculiar situation of the county would lead us to expect. "Shouldered out into the farthest part of the realm, and so besieged with the ocean, that, as a demi-island in an island, the inhabitants find but one way of issue by land,"‡ it is not surprising that, as in the case of the Roman occupation of our island, Cornwall should have again been the last part of England that submitted to the English conquest. Eastern Damnonia § —a name which we still seem to recognize in that of beautiful Devon — necessarily submitted before her western neighbour; but at last even the Cornish, in the early part of the 10th century, notwithstanding their having from time to time received help from Danish allies —afterwards their plunderers—were subjugated by Athelstan, who is said to have passed right through "West Wales" in 926, and again in 928, fixing the Tamar for the Cornish military frontier. It is nevertheless noticeable that, *west* of the Tamar, a tract, roughly included

* An interesting attempt to show the traces of Roman occupation in Cornwall has been made by Mr. Whitley. See 'Journal of Royal Institution of Cornwall.'
† It is interesting to note that there is also a district of Brittany called Cornouaille, teeming with Cornish names, and whose rustics are, moreover, celebrated wrestlers.
‡ Carew.
§ Perhaps the Latin form of Dyfnaint—the land of dark valleys.

between that river and a line drawn westward from about
Antony to Tintagel, contains many names distinctly of
Saxon origin—a fact which seems to indicate that at
least this portion of what is now called *Cornwall*, was,
from a still more remote period—perhaps as early as the
middle of the 7th century—in Saxon occupation.

To this comparatively late conquest of their soil, the
men of the West were fortunately indebted for a much
milder treatment by their victors than most of their
fellow-countrymen had previously received. The Cornish
were Christians before their conquerors; but the English
had gradually become christianized also, and the Christian Welsh could now sit down with the Christian Saxon;
no longer, as Dr. Freeman has observed, wild beasts,
enemies, or slaves, but fellow-citizens, living under the
king's peace. It is still the grateful boast of the county
that along her roadsides are plentifully dispersed those
imperishable stone crosses,* which, by their equal-limbed
Greek form, attest the primitive source from which she
derived her Christianity. To these early times must be
referred the origin of such stories as those of King
Arthur, of whose existence no Cornish man at least can
ever permit himself to doubt, though many a long year
was to roll by before "the blameless king" appeared in
a written chronicle.

As Cornwall preserved for a longer period than any
other part of England her political independence, so did
she also maintain her separate ecclesiastical standing.
More than two centuries elapsed between the adoption
of the Roman Easter by the King of Damnonia and the
submission of the Cornish bishop (with, possibly, the exception of Kenstec, in 833–70) to the Roman occupant of
the see of Canterbury, in A.D. 931; indeed it was not until
950 that Ethelgar, the first *English* bishop of Cornwall,
was appointed to Bodmin.†

We must pass rapidly by the ravages of the Danes in
the 11th century, though they were numerous and de-
structive, especially that of 1068. There is reason to sup-

* On the backs of many of these monuments Latin crosses
have been incised by later hands.

† It has been stated that Christianity was introduced into
Cornwall in the 2nd century; and it is known that there were
three British bishops at the Council of Ariminum in A.D. 359.
The Welsh Triads say that Cornwall was the seat of an arch-
bishop.

pose that traces of these rough times are still to be found in some of the hill and cliff castles.

But the dispossessor of the Celt was himself soon to be dispossessed for a time by the followers of the Norman conqueror; although nearly two years passed by before the two western counties submitted to William's rule, and the major part of the westernmost of them was allotted to the builder of our Norman-Cornish castles, Robert de Mortain, the conqueror's half-brother. The vitality of the Celtic proprietor, and the tenacity of his grasp of the soil (though nearly all traces of British customs, except perhaps the courts of the Stannaries, were swept away by the Saxons) are remarkably displayed under this double confiscation; for although the names of a few Norman landowners linger, even down to modern times, the majority of them died out at a comparatively early period; and the men of that soil from which their names were derived, "emerged from the débris of Norman and Saxon."

"By Tre, Ros, Pol, Lan, Caer, and Pen,
You may know* most Cornishmen,"

as Camden puts it; and Dr. Bannister has enumerated no less than 2400 Cornish proper names with Tre (= homestead), 500 with Pen (= head), 400 with Ros (= moor), 300 with Lan (= church or enclosure), 200 with Pol (= pool), and 200 with Caer (= town or camp). There are probably many more than this number.† It has been suggested that to the early and rapid decay of Norman feudalism in Cornwall may be due that lack of feudal

---

* The extent to which Cornish surnames are derived from the names of places is remarkable. There are several places in various parts of the county bearing the same name as the writer of this handbook; and that such names date from an early period is evident from the fact that one Nicholas Tregellas witnessed a deed at Lostwithiel in the reign of Edward II., and another— Thomas—was returned to Parliament as one of the members for Truro, in Richard II.'s third Parliament, at Westminster. Of course such names were probably in existence at a much earlier date; and it may here be observed that down to the middle of the last century Cornish gentlemen not only derived their names from their residences, but even changed the one with the other when they moved.

† It has often been observed that a large number of the names of Cornish parishes bear the prefix "Saint." Lysons gives a long list of ancient names without this prefix.

notions and that impatience of aristocratic interference,
which have always characterized the Cornish, and which
caused those great risings of the people which constitute
some of the main features of the county history.

Not to lay too much stress upon the disturbances
created by a few Lancastrian partisans in 1471, the risings
which occurred during the Tudor dynasty next deserve
a passing notice. The first of any importance—known
as Flammock's (or Flamaak's) rebellion — was in the
reign of Henry VII. (1495), whose exactions for the ex-
penses of the Scotch war raised a spirit of resistance
amongst the Cornishmen; which, afterwards aided perhaps
by a sympathy with the claims of Perkin Warbeck, who
landed on Cornish ground, resulted in "the most for-
midable danger which ever threatened Henry's throne."
But the bills and bows of the Cornish, though their arrows
were (says Lord Bacon) "the length of a tailor's yard,
so strong and mighty a bow were they said to draw," *
were no match for the king's artillery, which completed
their defeat at Blackheath. "Perkin's rebellion," in the
following year, ended very summarily in the submission
of his followers to Henry VII. at Exeter, and the committal of the pretender to the Tower.

The next rising—known as "Arundel's rebellion"—
was fifty years afterwards, when the Cornishmen, ever
averse to change, and now incited by Roman Catholic
priests, rose in a futile attempt for the defence of the
"old religion." Their leader was Humphry Arundel,
who mustered 10,000 "stout traitors," as Foxe calls them,
at St. Michael's Mount, but they were dispersed at Clifton
Downs on 19th August, 1549.†

It is scarcely necessary to add that the Reformed
faith ultimately prevailed ; and that, owing to the zealous
labours of Wesley towards the close of the last century
(which the Bishop of Truro in his recent first charge
bade his clergy "remember joyfully"), the general
tendency of religious thought in later times, at least
among the lower orders, has been, until recently, rather
towards dissent ; but it is curious to observe how, notwithstanding, most of the parishes retain the names of
their patron saints instead of the older secular names.

---

* 'Life of Henry VII.'
† Cf. Lord Clarendon's 'History of the Rebellion.'

Even more memorable than the foregoing incidents of Cornish history is the attitude which the county assumed during the Civil Wars. This was, no doubt, partly owing to a refusal of the House of Commons to redress certain Cornish grievances.* "Nowhere," says Mr. Green, in his 'Short History of the English People,' "was the Royal cause to take so brave or noble a form as among the Cornishmen. Cornwall stood apart from the general life of England : cut off from it not only by difference of blood and speech, ... they suffered their fidelity to the Crown to determine their own. They had as yet done little more than keep the war out of their own county; but the march of a small Parliamentary force, under Lord Stamford, upon Launceston, forced them into action. A little band of Cornishmen gathered round the chivalrous Sir Bevil Greenvil (*sic*), so destitute of provisions that the best officers had but a biscuit a day, and with only a handful of powder for the whole force; but, starving and outnumbered as they were, they scaled the steep rise of Stratton Hill,† sword in hand, and drove Stamford back to Exeter, with a loss of 2000 men, his ordnance and baggage train. Sir Ralph Hopton, the best of the Royalist generals, took command of their army as it advanced into Somerset, and drew the stress of the war into the west. Essex despatched a picked force, under Sir William Waller, to check their advance; but Somerset was already lost ere he reached Bath, and the Cornishmen stormed his strong position on Lansdown Hill in the teeth of his guns." Equal honours fell to their share at the siege of Bristol; and such services as these to the Royal cause could not be forgotten. They produced from Charles I.‡ a memorable letter of thanks to the county, dated Sudeley Castle, 10th September, 1643, in which he directs that a

* For full particulars, see Sir Richard Baker's 'Chronicle' (ed. Phillips, 1674, pp. 243, 244, and 304).

† A previous victory over the Parliamentary forces was obtained on Broadoak, or Bradock Down, on January 19, 1643.

‡ A declaration of King James I. was published in 1613, to the effect that Prince Charles was to be Duke of Cornwall on the death of the king's " first-begotten " son Henry. It may also be noted here, in further explanation of the strong feeling which existed on the part of the Cornish towards Charles I., that in the earlier part of his reign a Bill passed the Commons for making all the Cornish rivers navigable.

copy of it should be kept for ever in all the Cornish churches and chapels, " that, as long as the history of these times and of this nation shall continue, the memory of how much that county hath merited from us and our Crown may be derived with it to posterity." In many churches large copies of this epistle still hang on the walls, but from others they have been allowed to disappear.

Since those stirring times the history of Cornwall is the history of England; partly owing, no doubt, to the distance of this county from the great centres of political life. It has, so far as its individual history is concerned, mainly consisted in the peaceful and energetic development of her mineral and agricultural resources. The former, however, have, within the last few years, received a terrible blow from the discovery of vast quantities of tin and copper abroad—found under such favourable conditions as almost to preclude all hopes of Cornish competition. About three-fourths of the mines have been stopped; whilst in those that are still worked, only half the hands are employed, and those at reduced wages. Emigration of the working men has consequently taken place, to an enormous extent,

> " to distant climes, a dreary scene,
> Where half the convex world intrudes between."

The busy scenes where thousands of both sexes were once employed in the many varieties of mining operations are now nearly all deserted; a terrible poverty, which no "national subscription" has attempted to relieve, has found its way into many a humble home, and the face of the country is entirely changed.* Amidst all this distress a curious trait of Cornish character has appeared in certain discussions at public meetings held during the winter of 1877, when it was proposed to alleviate the sufferings of the mining population by the distribution of about 1000l., the balance of a sum collected for a similar purpose in 1867. The difficulty was this—the worthy poor

---

* There was a complaint of the decay of the population of Cornwall in the middle of the 16th century, and an Act of Parliament was passed in 1540 for the reconstruction of dwelling-houses in the towns of Truro, Bodmin, Launceston, Liskeard, Lostwithiel, and others.

could not be induced to own their poverty. The future progress of Cornwall must in all human probability depend upon some industry which shall replace that of which she has of late years been so completely deprived. Whether this is to be found in some profitable method of cultivating the vast tracts of moorland—in certain classes of agricultural and horticultural pursuits for which the climate is so singularly fitted, and for which the vast supplies of blown sand and seaweed afford manures—or from the further development of the fisheries (with their attendant industries), which exist at many parts of the long line of seaboard—or possibly from the establishment of local manufactories of porcelain, the natural ingredients of which exist under the soil in such inexhaustible abundance—remains to be seen.* It is well known that many mines increase in richness the deeper they are excavated, and it would be even yet more remarkable if the strenuous endeavours which are being made to improve the machinery used in deep-mining operations should succeed ; or if an increased demand for the products of the mines should arise, and so cause a repetition of that chapter of Cornish history which, for the last century and a half, has chiefly distinguished her as a county—her varied *mineral* wealth.

Finally, the most recent event of importance in the history of Cornwall has been the re-establishment of its ancient British bishopric, and the elevation of Truro to the dignity of a city, by letters patent, dated 28th August, 1877.

CLIMATE.

The climate of Cornwall, owing to the peculiar situation of the promontory, is so remarkable as to deserve special notice ; and to this subject Mr. Whitley has given

* It would be difficult to do more than justice in acknowledging the extreme value of the contributions of Mr. Whitley, of Truro, towards a correct appreciation of the geological, meteorological, and agricultural resources of his native county. Mr. Whitley's suggestive papers on these subjects are chiefly to be found in the journals of the Royal Institution of Cornwall, of the Royal Agricultural Society of England, &c., &c. The writer takes this opportunity of acknowledging how much he is indebted to these extensive and varied researches.

such long and careful attention that it would be difficult to do better than to quote his words.*

"A Canadian would think there was no summer, and say there was no winter; a Spaniard would wonder what had become of the sun; and a Peruvian would think it always rained.

"The month of January at Penzance is as warm as at Madrid, Florence, and Constantinople; and July is as cool as at St. Petersburg in that month. The seasons appear to mingle like the interlacing of the warm and cold waters on the edge of the Gulf-stream; and along our coast-line in January night and day have hardly a distinctive temperature, the mean difference being scarcely *four* degrees. There is no country in the world with a climate so mild and equable as the south-west of England, if we except the south-west of Ireland, where this peculiarity is intensified.

"The cause is now well understood. The Atlantic Ocean on the west is an immense reservoir of warm water, fed and heated by the Gulf-stream, so that around the Cornish lands in the depth of winter the temperature of the surface-water is seldom lower than 46°; and out at sea, beyond the influence of the land, the water is much warmer. The air pressed on its surface partakes of its temperature, and this warm air is swept by the prevailing westerly winds over the land, imparting to it the heat which was generated in and conveyed from the torrid zone. Let the cold be ever so intense in winter, the westerly wind will drive it back, and day after day the thermometer will stand at 50°.

"There is a magic touch and a mighty power about this brave west wind, which in winter we should thankfully acknowledge. In the middle of December, 1859, the cold from the north-east had coated Cornwall with snow, and loaded the trees and hedgerows with masses of glittering crystals. A falling barometer indicated that the generous hero of the west was approaching; his first blast was cold and chilly; but on, on, roaring and groaning, he came; sighing through the trees and hedge-

* 'Development of the Agricultural Resources of Cornwall,' 'Bath and West of England Agricultural Journal,' vol. ix. part 2. *Cf.* Mr. Whitley's 'Prize Essay on the Climate of the British Islands,' 'Journal of the Royal Agricultural Society,' 1850.

rows, and the snow fell in heavy lumps from the boughs. From the western sides of hills, and from the more exposed brows of the land, the snow melted rapidly away, and so effective was his influence that lines of temperature might almost be drawn on the delicately-shaded surface. Within twenty-four hours the white mantle of winter was gone, and the emerald green of spring returned, except that here and there were left some patches of snow which had skulked under the eastern side of a hedge ; and the thermometer ranged from 50° at night to 54° by day.

"But in *summer* admiration changes into dislike. 'Fair weather may come out of the north,' but the tyrant of the west rolls in, cloud on cloud, till the sun is obscured by masses of vapour which, day after day, no ray of his can pierce ; then long pendent streams of condensing vapour float over the languishing ears of corn, or descend in heavy rain to retard and injure the harvest. The sun may be a monarch in the desert, where 'the earth is fire and the sun is flame,' but in Cornwall we often view him as the 'dim discrowned god of day,' and long to feel more of his vivifying beams, gilding the fading corn and swelling the half-ripe fruit."

Humboldt calculated that, according to the latitude of England, it should have an annual rainfall of 22 inches (about 2200 tons per acre). As a matter of fact, however, the English average is half as much again; whilst Cornwall gets a double share, or 44 inches annually.

The flora and fauna of the county are therefore, owing to the mildness of the climate, to a considerable extent of a sub-tropical character. To enumerate the various interesting examples which have been noticed would unduly increase the contents of this handbook; but those who are curious in the matter will find ample details, in a most attractive form, in the 'Reports of the Royal Institution of Cornwall.' * To attempt to give them here would neither do justice to the naturalist nor to Cornwall.

For the invalid suffering from chest or throat complaints the well-known advantages of the climate of the south of Cornwall are greater than those of any other part of the kingdom.

* The Meteorological Tables kept by the Curator, and the 'Ornithology,' by Mr. E. H. Rodd, are particularly copious and valuable.

THE PEOPLE.

Truism though it be, that race and situation determine the character of a people, yet the Cornish are so peculiar in both respects, that in Cornwall this should always be borne in mind. Their Celtic blood * makes them ardent and vivacious ; their almost insulated position has caused them to be self-reliant and versatile. It is no uncommon thing for a Cornish man to build his own house, make his own shoes, and be both fisherman and miner—possibly a small shopkeeper besides.

But his character shall be pourtrayed by the impartial pens of strangers.

Queen Elizabeth said that " the Cornish gentlemen were all born courtiers, with a becoming confidence." A close observer of character, Mr. Wilkie Collins, writes :—
" As a body of men they are industrious and intelligent, sober and orderly ; neither soured by hard work, nor easily depressed by harsher privations. . . . . The views of the working men are remarkably moderate and sensible. I never met with so few grumblers anywhere." The tourist will almost invariably find them courteous and hospitable, most willing to impart whatever information they can, and equally ready to receive any facts (especially of a personal nature) in return ; but any curt reply or haughty demeanour on the part of the visitor will at once prove fatal to agreeable intercommunications. A London pedestrian in 1649 writes—
" Cornwall is the compleate and repleate Horne of Abundance, for high churlish hills, and affable, courteous people. . . . . The country hath its share of huge stones, mighty rocks, noble free gentlemen, bountiful housekeepers, strong and stout men, handsome and beautiful women." Warner, in his ' Tour through Cornwall,' in 1808, says —" Its men are sturdy, bold, honest, and sagacious; its women lovely and modest, courteous and unaffected." Their courage is sufficiently evidenced by their gallant conduct during the Civil Wars, when they are said to have " twice rescued the Royal cause ; "—in 1643, by the victories at Stratton and Lansdown, and in 1644, at

* Professor Max Müller, in his ' Chips from a German Workshop,' ranks the Celt very high in the qualifications of " physical beauty and intellectual vigour."

Broadoak: how Lord Exmouth, a Penzance man, with
a crew of Cornish miners who had never before been
to sea, defeated a French frigate, may be read in his
biography by another Cornishman, the late Edward
Osler, F.R.S. Mr. J. O. Halliwell Phillips says:—"Yet
of all the attractions of Cornwall, surely the greatest is
the genial character of the people, which would almost
suffice to make a desert an agreeable place of sojourn to
a stranger. The same description of their courtesy holds
true at the present day. It is a rarity to find a native,
in however humble a condition, who does not display
that truest and best politeness which arises from an
anxious desire to satisfy an inquiry or a want." Diodorus
Siculus observed that "the people who inhabit a promontory of Britain called Bolerium, are exceedingly
hospitable and courteous in their manners." Festus
Avienus says of them—

> " . . . . multa vis hic gentis est,
> Superbus animus, efficax solertia,
> Negotiandi cura jugis omnibus."

And Leifchild, the author of 'Cornwall; its Mines and
Miners,' observes—" I would prefer a month's walk over
Cornish scenes, or a month's sojourn among Cornish
peasants, to the same anywhere else."

The only dark side which we have been able to find to
these pleasant pictures of the Cornish, as given by out-
siders, is that drawn by poor Lady Fanshawe, who, in
the midst of her sad troubles whilst passing through
Cornwall during the rebellion, observed that, though
"the gentlemen of this county are generally loyal to the
Crown and hospitable to their neighbours, yet they are
of a crafty and censorious nature, as most are so far from
London."

It must, moreover, be admitted that (whilst they are
imaginative and devotional) they are also often superstitious; especially as regards charms for the cure of
illness, and also as to fairies and pixies. In some parts of
Cornwall branches of seaweed are set up as ornaments in
the house to preserve it from fire: these are called
(? our) Lady's tresses. One notable instance of credulity
is that a stone celt—locally called a thunderbolt—is,
when boiled, a cure for rheumatism. Another is, that a

mutton knuckle - bone, a raw potato, or a loadstone, carried in the pocket is a cure for sciatica.

The men have usually a good physique, and are celebrated for the breadth of their shoulders. A Cornish militia regiment was observed at *Chatham* to require from this cause a greater area of ground than any other. With the exception of the miners, whose various illnesses, engendered by their dangerous and unhealthy pursuits, have formed the theme of many medical treatises by Dr. Barham and others, the inhabitants have been remarkable for their longevity. The peculiar, half-foreign beauty of many of the fairer sex in some districts has been a subject of remark from time immemorial.

Many curious old customs still linger in Cornwall. Among them may be mentioned the ceremony of " cutting the neck," or last few ears of corn, at harvest time; the lighting of bonfires on the hills, on St. John's eve; and the furry or Flora dance at Helston, on the 8th of May. Nor must we omit to mention some of the curious dishes peculiar to the Cornish *cuisine.* Pre-eminent is the pasty—the almost universal daily dinner of the working class—a savoury compound of meat and potatoes enclosed in a crescent-shaped crust; but it is necessary to be a Cornishman to *thoroughly* appreciate this dish. The variety of pies is truly marvellous, and most of them are richly saturated with clotted cream : such are veal and parsley, leeks, conger eels, and pilchards, whose heads peeping through the crust have earned for this dish the title of star-gazing pies. It has been said that the devil himself would be put into a pie if only he could be caught anywhere in Cornwall. This gave rise to the following scandalous lines, penned on an occasion when several Cornish attorneys, meeting at Quarter Sessions at a time when wheat was very scarce and dear, resolved to abstain from pastry :—

> " If the proverb is true that the fame of our pies
> Prevents us from falling to Satan a prey,
> It is clear that his friends the attorneys are wise
> In moving such obstacles out of the way."

There are plenty of old stories about wrecking and smuggling; and no doubt in former times a good deal of both went on in Cornwall as well as on other parts of the coast. If more were done in Cornwall than elsewhere it is easily accounted for by the dangerous and extended coast line. But the best vindication of Cornish manners and morals will be found in the creditable position which the county occupies in the Criminal Returns.

THE OLD CORNISH LANGUAGE.

An ancient tongue still used in the names of most of the *places* in the county, as well as in the names of many *things*, and which even lingers, in remote corners, in the form of rustic expressions now rapidly growing obsolete,— but yet occasionally breaking through the modern tongue, as Plutonic rocks force their way through superincumbent strata,—must be considered deserving of a short notice.

Though at the time of the departure of the Romans the language of which the Cornish is, or rather was, the representative, was that spoken over at least all southern Britain, its literary remains are confined to three or four MSS., the earliest of which, a vocabulary, dates from the 13th century, whilst of the remainder, mostly sacred dramas (probably not by a Cornish author), none is earlier than the 14th. The difficulties of understanding it are consequently very considerable, but, thanks to the learned labours of Edwin Norris,* whose translations of the Ancient Cornish Drama, together with grammar and vocabulary, were published about twenty years ago, a fair idea of the history and character of the language can even yet be gained.

The Cornish is, of course, a Celtic language—allied rather to the Welsh and Armoric branches than to the Irish, Scotch, and Manks. In short, it is Cymric, not Gaelic. Probably it is not of so early an origin as the Irish, but is older than the Welsh; an opinion for which Norris gives good reasons.

The language was sufficiently like the Welsh and Armoric for the Bretons and Welshmen to understand it, to some extent, when spoken; but, not to mention certain differences in its grammar and vocabulary, Scawen, writing at the close of the 17th century, says, its sound was not so *guttural* as the Welsh, nor *muttered* like the

* Scawen, Keigwyn, Llhuyd, Gwavas, and Pryce (Tonkin), are earlier authorities, but the most scientific treatise Norris considered to be Zeuss's ' Grammatica Celtica.'

c

Armoric; and Carew's description of it is somewhat
similar. Max Müller says of it that "it was a melodious
and yet by no means an effeminate language." Into the
causes of its decay it hardly seems necessary to enter
here, though Scawen gives no less than sixteen lengthy
and elaborate reasons for it. The same obvious causes
which are gradually exterminating Welsh in our own
days obliterated Cornish in the times of our ancestors.

Although it was pretty generally spoken in the days of
Henry VIII., Norden says (about 1584) that "the
Cornish men have much conformed themselves to the
English tongue;" adding that, in the west part of the
country, "the Cornish tongue is most in use amongst
the inhabitants . . . . yet there is none of them but in
a manner is able to converse with a stranger in the
English tongue, unless it be some obscure people that
seldom confer with the better sort." Carew says it had
fallen into disuse in 1602; but this statement requires
qualification, as Hals says that in 1640 the vicar of
Feock was obliged to administer the sacrament in
Cornish to his older parishioners. In 1644 it was the
rustic language of the Meneage, Pendennis, and Land's
End districts; and the last sermon in Cornish was not
preached till 1678 in Landewednack church. The guaries,
or miracle-plays, continued to be acted in Cornish for
some time afterwards.*

In 1701, Llhuyd writes that every Cornish man could
then speak English, and that Cornish was then spoken
only in a few villages in the Land's End district; and
Borlase says the fishermen in the western part of the
country used it pretty generally at the beginning of the
last century; though, he adds, the general use of it had
ceased in 1758. Yet Daines Barrington considered he
heard Dolly Pentreath speak it in 1768 at Mousehole,
as Borlase certainly did in 1774: in fact, Newlyn and
Mousehole appear to have been its last stronghold.
Pryce says, that in 1790 he knew an old man who could
speak it; and Whitaker (author of the 'Ancient Cathedral of Cornwall') heard of two persons who could speak
it, in 1799.

* Bishop Gibson, in his additions to Camden's 'Cornwall'
(1678–1700), says one of the disadvantages of suppressing the
Cornish language would be loss of commerce and correspondence
with the Armoricans of Brittany.

The "coup de grâce," however, was no doubt given in the 16th century, as to which Scawen writes: "Our people in Queen Elizabeth's time desired that the common liturgy should be in the *English* tongue, to which they were then for novelty's sake affected, not out of true judgment desired it." Dr. Moreman is said to have first introduced this innovation at Menheniot.

A slight specimen of the Cornish language may be interesting; and I have selected the following because I believe it is the only example extant of which even an approximation to the right pronunciation is certainly known. Norris gives it as having been taken down by him from the lips of an old man who had been taught, when a child, the Lord's Prayer and the Apostles' Creed in Cornish :—

"Dew an Tas Olgallosak"—"God, the Father Almighty," was pronounced, Duan taza gallasack; the *a's* sounded like *a* in father. The writer will, he hopes, be excused for adding, that, for illustrations of the ways in which many old Cornish words and phrases are still used by the miners and rural population generally,—as well as for a vivid pourtrayal of the manners and customs of the people, and the peculiar dialects of the various parts of the country,—the reader may be referred to several tales and sketches, both humorous and serious, contained in works of the late John Tabois Tregellas. He has the less hesitation in doing this, as they were commended to the attention of the British Archæological Association at Bodmin in 1876, by Mr. Stokes, the Clerk of the Peace for Cornwall.

For a scientific treatment of the subject the pages of the Philological Society's publications, especially a paper by Mr. Henry Jenner, in 1873, on the Cornish language at its various periods, may be advantageously consulted. Mr. Jenner has recently discovered a very early composition in the Cornish language (perhaps the earliest extant) on the back of an ancient charter preserved in the British Museum.

MINES.

(By RICHARD MEADE, Esq., of the Royal School of Mines.)

Cornwall, from time immemorial, has been intimately associated with the mineral and metallurgical industries of Britain; indeed, in no other county in the kingdom can

richer metalliferous deposits be found. The " Cassiterides " or Tin Islands of the historian have been thought
to be the Scilly Islands ; but, as there is no evidence that
any tin was ever found in Scilly, this idea must be relinquished. The name in all probability was given by
the early navigators to this most western part of England,
over which is spread the tin formations, and where we
find evidences of mine workings of the highest antiquity.

Diodorus Siculus, who wrote in the 1st century B.C.,
describes the trade with Cornwall, "Bolerion," for tin, and
mentions the place of shipment, in the following account :
" The inhabitants of that extremity of Britain which is
called Bolerion, both excel in hospitality, and also, by
reason of their intercourse with foreign merchants, are
civilized in their mode of life. These prepare the tin,
working very carefully the earth which produces it. The
ground is rocky, but it has in it earthy veins, the produce
of which is brought down and melted and purified. Then,
when they have cast it into the form of cubes, they carry
it to certain islands adjoining to Britain, and called Ictin.
During the recess of the tide, the intervening space is
left dry, and they carry over abundance of tin to these
places in their carts.   And it is something peculiar that
happens to the islands in these parts lying between Europe
and Britain ; for at full tide, the intervening passage
being overflowed, they appear islands, but when the sea
retires a large space is left dry, and they are seen as
peninsulas.   From hence then the traders purchase the
tin of the natives, and transport it to Gaul, and finally,
travelling through Gaul on foot, in about thirty days
bring their burden on horses to the mouth of the river
Rhone."   Some have supposed the Isle of Wight to be
the "Ictin," but it does not fulfil any of the conditions
of the geographer ; whereas, Saint Michael's Mount and
Looe Island, to which may also perhaps be added Drake's
Island in Plymouth Harbour, in all respects agree with the
description.

The earliest traders for tin with Cornwall are considered to have been the Phœnicians, who, from their
colony of Gades on the western coast of Spain, were the
medium of commercial intercourse between Phœnicia and
Cornwall.   It further appears that the traders in this

metal considered it so important that they concealed the situation whence it was obtained. As early as the 6th and 7th centuries, with the introduction of bells into the churches and cathedrals of Western Europe, a considerable demand for Cornish tin arose, and subsequently the sale was greatly increased by the use of cannon.

The principal emporium for the tin trade in the 13th century was Bruges; and later, the merchants of Italy obtained the tin of Cornwall and distributed it among the countries of the Levant, though Bruges at that time continued to be the great market for Cornish tin. According to Borlase, the produce of tin in Cornwall was inconsiderable in the time of King John (who granted a charter to the tinners of Cornwall and Devon), the property in the mines precarious and unsettled, and the tin traffic engrossed by the Jews to the great regret of the barons and their vassals, the right of working the tin being wholly in the king, as Earl of Cornwall. The tin-farm of Cornwall then only amounted to one hundred marks (66*l*. 13*s*. 4*d*.) per annum, while the tin of Devon was at the same time farmed for 100*l*.

Subsequently, in the time of Richard, Duke of Cornwall, the produce of the tin mines is described as being considerable, so that he derived great revenue from them; but after the banishment of the Jews in the 18th of Edward I., the mines were again neglected.

By charters of King John and Edward I., power was granted to the tinners to take both turf and wood for smelting their tin, as had been their ancient custom, so that then and previously both kinds of fuel were employed in the reduction of the ore.

During more than six centuries the tin paid a tax to the Earls and Dukes of Cornwall after being smelted, having been cast into blocks, that appear, judging from ancient specimens which have been found, to have varied in size and form, but which were latterly of a rectangular shape with a bevel, corresponding with the mould, between the upper and lower surfaces, and weighing 3·34 cwts. each. The tin, each block being marked with the smelter's stamp, was carried to certain towns for the purpose of being coined; that is, after having a corner of the blocks struck off and examined by Duchy officers appointed for the purpose (in order to see that the tin was of proper quality), the blocks were stamped with the Duchy seal, the dues paid, and the blocks permitted to be sold.

It appears by a charter of Edward I. (1305) to the Cornish tinners, that the coinage towns then appointed were Lostwithiel, Bodmin, Liskeard, Truro, and Helston; Penzance being added to the list in the reign of Charles II. In the year 1837 the coinages of the Duchy of Cornwall were effected at Calstock, St. Austell, Truro, Hayle, and Penzance.

In the year 1838, by an Act passed on the 16th August, the duties payable on the coinages of tin in Cornwall and Devon were abolished, and a compensation in lieu of them was given to the Duchy; and at the same time the duties on the imports of foreign tin were reduced, and at a later period entirely remitted.

The varied operations succeeding each other, and employed in obtaining the ores, and their subsequent conversion in the furnace to the metallic form, is too large a subject to be considered here. It will therefore be convenient first to refer generally to the rocks in which the several minerals are found, and their order of occurrence, following with Returns of production, showing quantities and values, and concluding with such facts as may prove interesting to the general reader, e.g. as depths of mines, accidents, and the mining population.

Cornwall, geologically, presents several large surfaces of granite, protruding through other rocks known as killas or clay-slate. The general direction of these granite masses is from W.S.W. to E.N.E. The granite is intrusive, as the killas is found to repose upon it at an angle of about 45°. In these granite and killas rocks occur veins or lodes bearing metalliferous minerals; these mineral veins run nearly parallel; sometimes a series of veins are seen in two directions at nearly right angles bearing tin and copper.* The character of metalliferous ores is generally marked by their direction. Mineral

---

* Roughly speaking, tin and copper lodes run east and west, and lead lodes north and south. Tin is mostly found in the granite, and has been most abundant in the St. Austell and St. Agnes neighbourhoods. The Gwennap, Redruth, and Camborne districts have produced the most copper; whilst lead, antimony, and manganese are chiefly found in the slaty rocks of north-east Cornwall.—W. H. T.

veins are subject to great interruptions in their course, both laterally and vertically, from the nature of the rock through which they pass. In passing from a granite to a bedded rock they are generally deflected, and when this takes place, the mineral deposit is found to diminish.

Numbers of our deepest mines have at times been abandoned from the veins having become small; though when at a subsequent period operations have been further extended, they have proved a rich harvest to the adventurer. Mineral lodes are sometimes cut through by other veins, known as cross-courses. Boase, in referring to these, says: "When these granitic veins are of a large size, they are termed elvan courses; indeed, this is the only distinction between these two forms of elongated masses of granite rock." These elvans are composed of quartziferous porphyry, that is, a granular crystalline mixture of felspar and quartz, and are common in both Cornwall and Devonshire. Generally, these elvan courses are considered favourable for the discovery of tin and copper; while, on the other hand, when the granite in which they occur is found sufficiently compact for building purposes (for which it is largely employed) the conditions for mining are seldom favourable.

The killas or clay-slate previously referred to is the rock in which most lodes occur;—a white variety is considered favourable for mining, and is invariably selected by miners. When of a pale grey or buff colour, but more especially when the killas assumes a bluish tinge, the mineral vein becomes impoverished. In some of the western mines, at the junction of the granite and slate, the killas-bearing vein is found to pass from one kind of ore to another; but where a vein passes from one rock to another, the mineral is not found equally rich in each rock.

Tin is invariably found in the crystalline and metamorphic rocks, in several forms of deposit, the more important of which is in veins or lodes; and from such the great bulk of tin annually obtained in Cornwall is derived. It also occurs in the form of stream tin, i.e., in small grains and nodules, deposited in alluvial sands and gravels, the result of the disintegration of the primary rocks of the neighbouring hills. All the operations of the early tinners were directed to these deposits; and stream works, until late in the last century, furnished the chief supply of tin.

Tin is almost exclusively obtained from cassiterite or tin-stone, a peroxide of tin containing nearly 80 per cent. of the metal, and is readily separated from most of its accompanying minerals, by taking advantage of the great density of the ore.

Production of Metallic (White) *Tin.*—In the reigns of James I. and Charles I. the yield of metallic tin varied from 1400 to 1600 tons. 2100 tons was the yield in 1742, and this was the average produce for several years. The following are the quantities produced in each of the years named :—

Year.	Tons.	Year.	Tons.
1760	2717	1800	2522
1770	2977	1810	2006
1780	2926	1820	2775
1790	3193	1830	4183

The average price of metallic tin per cwt. in 1780 was 3*l*. 8*s*., increasing to 5*l*. 1*s*. in 1800, and 7*l*. 17*s*. in 1810, when prices fell to 3*l*. 13*s*. 6*d*. in 1820, and 3*l*. 12*s*. in 1830; when it again increased in value until 1836, realising 5*l*. 9*s*. 6*d*. per cwt.

The following account shows the number of blocks coined; distinguishing the quantity coined in each coinage town in both counties, and the grain tin from common tin, in the year from Midsummer, 1837, to Midsummer, 1838, when coining was abolished.

Coinage Towns.	Grain Tin.	Common Tin.	Total.
Calstock	..	393	393
Truro	1,345	8,952	10,297
Hayle	118	5,334	5,452
Penzance	..	12,423	12,423
Totals	1,463	27,102	28,565

In the same year the tin imported into the United Kingdom amounted to 1451 tons, while the exports amounted to 1465 tons.

Referring to the "Mineral Statistics of the United Kingdom," first issued for the year 1848, the production of tin (black) ore amounted to 10,176 tons, increased to 10,383 tons in the year 1850, and receding to 9674 tons in the year 1852, and still further in the year 1854 to 8747 tons, of which quantity about 300 tons were raised in Devonshire; the average price of the black tin being 64*l.* per ton, giving a total value of 559,808*l.*; while the black tin in 1854 yielded on smelting from 67 to 68 per cent. of metallic (white) tin, equivalent to 5947 tons; the average prices of the several varieties of metal the same year being, English blocks, 114*l.* per ton; bars, 115*l.*, and refined, 118*l.* per ton.

The extent and importance of mining operations in the production of tin alone in Cornwall and Devonshire will be understood by the following abstract, showing the number of mines selling black tin, the quantity produced, and its average value in each of the years given.

Year.	Number of Mines.	Price of Ore per Ton.		Tin Ore.	
				Quantity.	Value.
		£ *s.* *d.*		tons	£
1858	137	63 4 0		9,959	633,501
1860	143	71 11 6		10,400	812,160
1862	147	59 14 0		11,841	777,396
1864	174	60 17 6		13,985	881,031
1866	145	48 10 0		13,785	667,999
1868	109	55 4 0		11,584	641,137
1870	147	75 3 0		15,234	1,002,357
1872	162	87 7 0		14,266	1,246,135
1874	230	56 3 0		14,039	788,310
1876	135	43 18 0		13,688	600,923

The unfavourable condition of the tin industries appears in the low price of the ore in 1876, compared with 1872, when the value was 87*l.* 7*s.* per ton; indeed, in the history of Cornish mining, a more discouraging state of affairs has never occurred.

To compare the metallic (white) tin produced in each of the above years is appended the following abstract of quantities produced and values; also side by side is given the average price per ton of common block tin in each of the same years.

Year.	Metallic Tin.		Price per Ton.		
	Quantity.	Value.			
	tons	£	£	s.	d.
1858	6,491	772,429	119	2	2
1860	6,656	866,306	136	3	1
1862	7,578	879,048	116	0	0
1864	9,295	995,029	107	1	0
1866	8,822	781,849	88	12	6
1868	7,703	756,494	98	0	0
1870	10,200	1,299,505	127	8	6
1872	9,560	1,459,990	152	15	0
1874	9,942	1,077,712	108	8	0
1876	8,500	675,750	79	10	2

Since the year 1872, the price of metallic tin has thus declined from 152l. 15s. to 79l. 10s. in the year 1876; a fact in itself showing the disadvantage under which mining operations are being carried on.

Many of the mines of Cornwall have, with occasional interruptions, been in operation for upwards of a century; but, interesting as it would be to refer to the history of some of the more important, space renders it desirable that our reference should be confined to one example, namely, Botallack, in the extreme west of Cornwall. This mine was originally worked as a tin mine from the year 1721, under a perpetual grant from the Boscawen family, but was relinquished in 1835. It is not precisely known when it was first worked for copper, but about the year 1816 it was one of the richest tin mines in the county. When the sett was relinquished in 1835, the mine had become very poor; yet in the thirty-four years ending at that date, the adventurers had made a profit of upwards of 30,000l.! The mine was again on the point of being abandoned in 1841, when it was determined to make further explorations for a period of two months, which resulted in the discovery of a very rich copper lode, yielding the adventurers a profit of 24,000l. within the twelve months! Since 1841 the mine has yielded considerable returns of both tin and copper, and was worked for 2448 feet under the sea for copper until the end of 1875, when the under-sea workings were abandoned. The mine is now worked as a tin mine once more.

Tin.

The earliest returns available for tin ore are for the year 1853. In the annexed statement appears the tin produce and value in each of the following years:—

Year.	Tin Ore.		Value.		
	tons	cwt.	£	s.	d.
1853	147	9	8,656	16	0
1856	148	19	13,285	9	1
1859	153	1	12,308	5	11
1862	354	0	24,508	5	9
1865	390	2	22,107	8	1
1868	375	6	21,381	14	3
1869	525	4	38,268	12	11
1871	497	14	39,552	0	9
1873	352	9	12,303	6	0
1875	358	6	18,556	4	1
1876	323	0	14,318	0	0

The value of tin ore has fallen considerably during the past four years; in 1872 it rose to 87l. 7s. per ton, since which time it has fallen to 78l. 1s. in 1873; to 52l. 11s. 6d. in 1875; and 43l. 18s. in 1876. In 1877 there has been an advance of about 10l. per ton.

With the development of the copper and tin mines of Cornwall in depth, the application of powerful machinery became necessary to drain the underground workings. Examples of the pumping engines may be seen at work in all the mining districts of the county. The depth of a few of the mines will point to the magnitude of the mechanical arrangements necessary. At Botallack mine, in Saint Just, the workings are at a depth of 250 fathoms from the sea level, or 1500 feet; and the levels are driven 2448 feet under the sea; while in mines in other districts, the following depths have been attained:—

Mines.	District.	Fathoms.	Feet.
Carn Brea	.. Illogan ..	.. 315 =	1890
Consolidated ..	.. Gwennap ..	.. 312	1872
Cooks Kitchen ..	.. Illogan ..	.. 340	2040
Dolcoath	.. Camborne ..	.. 371	2226
Tresavean	.. Gwennap ..	.. 350	2100

Copper.

The early history of copper mining in this country is somewhat obscure. Copper was worked at a remote period in Anglesea by the Romans; in Cumberland, near Keswick; and at Ecton, in Staffordshire, in 1670: but although copper was known at an early period in Cornwall it was only valued on account of the precious metals it was supposed to contain. Borlase says that, up to the end of the 17th century, Cornish miners knew very little of the true value of copper ore; and that some merchants from Bristol made it their business to inspect our mines more narrowly, and bought the copper raised for 2l. 10s. per ton! The yellow ore, which now sells for a price between 10l. and 20l. per ton, was at that time called *poder* (that is, dust), and was thrown away as mundic. The production of copper ore in 1775 was 27,896 tons, value, 189,609l., and yielding of metallic copper, 3347 tons. This quantity gradually increased until the year 1789, when the production of ore was 33,281 tons, value 184,308l.

About this period, 1789, considerable agitation spread through the mines of Cornwall by the infringement of Boulton and Watt's patent for their improved pumping engine, the consequence of which was a desire to keep secret as much as possible the proceedings at the mines. This resulted in the returns of production not being published for several years.

In the annexed table appear the quantities of ore raised, the metallic copper produced, and its value, in each of the following years from Cornish and Devonshire mines:—

Year.	Copper Ore.	Metallic Copper.	Value of Ore.
	tons	tons	£
1794	42,816	..	320,875
1800	55,981	5,187	550,925
1815	78,483	6,525	552,813
1830	133,904	10,748	773,846
1845	162,557	12,883..	919,934
1850	155,025	12,253.	840,410
1860	180,883	11,797..	1,071,063
1870	81,278	5,606.	326,322

Since 1870 a gradual falling off in production has taken place, the average price of the ore showing an increase from 4*l*. 13*s*. 6*d*, per ton in 1872, to 5*l*. per ton in 1875, but receding in 1876 to 4*l*. 17*s*. per ton.

The produce of the Cornish mines for copper during the past five years appears in the following table, with the number of mines and value of ore and metal.

Year.	No. of Mines.	Copper Ore.		Metallic Copper.	
		Quantity.	Value.	Quantity.	Value.
		tons	£	tons	£
1872	63	41,756	226,654	2,943	306,757
1873	68	40,285	188,236	2,973	285,110
1874	78	40,455	201,307	2,770	249,263
1875	67	39,393	204,228	2,698	242,815
1876	65	43,016	202,203	3,034	252,757

Lead.

Lead Mines.—The ores of lead were first wrought in Cornwall in the early part of the last century. Borlase records the working of but one mine in 1758, and even in 1839 the production did not exceed 180 tons, while some years later, from 1845 to 1850, the annual production increased to upwards of 10,000 tons, the most productive mine being East Wheal Rose, yielding from 3000 to 4000 tons of metallic lead. This mine, however, has long ceased to be worked owing to its being flooded. The yield of the Cornish lead mines has also greatly diminished in recent years, the returns for the three years ending 1876 being as follows:—

	1874.	1875.	1876.
	tons	tons	tons
Lead ore	3,120	2,556	2,727
Lead	2,337	1,932	2,070
	oz.	oz.	oz.
*Silver	85,304	25,681	37,650

* Gold has sometimes been found in small quantities, generally in stream works.—W. H. T.

The average prices of lead ore were 14*l*. 13*s*. 6*d*. in 1874, compared with 15*l*. 9*s*. 3*d*. in 1875, and 15*l*. 8*s*. in

1876; the prices of pig lead in each of the same years being respectively 22*l*. 2*s*., 22*l*. 9*s*. 4*d*., and 21*l*. 13*s*. 10*d*.

Zinc.

Zinc Ores.—These ores are raised in considerable quantities in Cornwall, amounting to 20 per cent. in the year 1876 of all raised in the United Kingdom; the ores are principally sulphide of zinc (black jack). The total yield of fourteen mines was 4414 tons, of the value of 14,593*l*., the ore yielding an average of 28 per cent. of metallic zinc. By far the greatest bulk of the zinc raised in Cornwall in 1876 was derived from West Chiverton Mine, in the parish of Perranzabuloe, which produced 3004 tons, valued at 10,514*l*.

Pyrites, &c.

Pyrites (*Mundic*; *Sulphur and Arsenical Ores*).—Upwards of 16 per cent. of these ores for the year 1876 was furnished by sixteen Cornish mines; the quantities sold amounting to 8243 tons, valued at 14,915*l*.

Miscellaneous.

Of other metalliferous ores and clays, the following abstract shows the quantities and values of each variety obtained in the year 1876.

Minerals.	Quantities.	Value.
	tons	£
Iron ores	18,390	10,566
Arsenic *	2,557	12,662
	cwt. qr. lb.	
Bismuth and Cobalt	7 3 18	†
Uranium	Some raised.	Not sold.
	tons	
Wolfram	23½	173
Silver and Copper Precipitate ...	1	..
Manganese	2,666	9,243
Porcelain, or Kaolin	34,500	†
Other Clays	390	†
Barytes	696	570

* In December, 1877, the price of best white powdered Cornish arsenic was £8 15*s*. per ton.—W. H. T.

† Value not returned. In December, 1877, the price varied from 15*s*. to 34*s*. for china clay, according to quality.—W. H. T.

Mining Population.

The total number of persons employed in the mines of Cornwall under inspection in the year 1876, was 18,632, of all ages ; of these 9781 were engaged in operations under ground, and 8851 above ground.

The numbers employed in Cornish mines in each of the preceding years were as follows :—

	1873.	1874.	1875.
Under ground ..	13,519	11,588	10,334
Above ,, ..	13,009	10,529	9,190
Totals	26,528	22,117	19,524

R. M.

A mine (though one *must* be inspected to be understood) may be roughly described as a set of excavations in the earth—some vertical (shafts), some horizontal (levels and adits)—in search of minerals: admirable models are to be seen at the Museum of Practical Geology in Jermyn Street. *Pumps*, worked by magnificent steam engines (of which probably the best in the world are made in Cornwall),* are necessary for draining the lower levels; the pumping engines are also occasionally employed to assist the men in going and returning from the depths of the mines. Other machines, such as *whims*, are employed in drawing the ore to the surface; *stamps* are used for crushing the ore which has previously been "*spalled*," or broken into small pieces; and "*buddles*," "*trunks*," and many another oddly named apparatus are employed for separating the useful from the useless portions. The "dressed" ore is deposited on the "*sampling floors*," from which samples of the various heaps are sent to the assayers of the different copper merchants, to enable them to fix the price which they consider to be its value, and to bid for the parcels of ores accordingly at the periodical auctions known as "*ticketings*." The tin ores are smelted in Cornwall, but most of the copper ores are sent to Swansea. Some of the men, "*tut-workers*,"

* The first steam engine in Cornwall is said to have been erected at Huel Vor, between 1710 and 1714. Newcomen, Watt, Hornblower, Woolf, and Trevithick severally developed this invaluable auxiliary to mining enterprise.

are paid daily wages, or by the job; others work on
"*tribute*," i. e. they pay so much in the £ for being
allowed to work the "lodes." A few years ago, according to Leifchild ('Cornwall; its Mines and Miners'*), the
average earnings of the tributer were 58s. 3d. per month,
and those of a tut-worker 53s. 8d. Babbage considered
the "*tribute*" system, and the co-operative principle
adopted in the Cornish fisheries, as admirable arrangements for both employers and employed.

Mines are usually worked by companies of adventurers,
who lease the "*sett*," as it is called, for a term of years,
paying the lord of the soil a royalty ("*the lord's dish*") on
the ores sold, which averages 1-15th. Mining in Cornwall has always been a most speculative pursuit;—many
persons have been ruined by it; whilst, on the other hand,
a few have made large fortunes. The profits made by a
few of the richer mines in the Gwennap district alone have
been stated as follows, namely,—

	£
Huel Bassett	100,000
„ Chance	150,000
„ Music	100,000
„ Spinster	80,000
„ Treskirby	200,000
„ Camborne Vean	200,000
„ Great Wheal Towan	250,000

The *Stannary Courts* (from *stannum* = tin), dating from
about the middle of the 13th century (and, in a simpler
form, much earlier), are specially devoted to the mining
interest; and miners claim to be free from all other
jurisdiction, except in matters affecting land, life, or limb.

The Prince of Wales, as Duke of Cornwall (the Duchy
was created in 1337), is Lord Warden; the Vice-Warden,
who acts as judge, is generally some barrister of eminence.
He presides at the court held periodically at Truro,
where the last "Stannary Parliament" was held in 1752.
The early Stannators used to meet on Hingston Down.

Such is a very brief outline of this branch of the
subject; it is after all but an amplification of what is contained in perhaps the oldest book in the world; for Job
says (chapter xxviii.):—" Iron is taken out of the earth,
and brass is molten out of the stone. He setteth an end

* A full and popular work on the subject.

to darkness, and searcheth out all perfection: the stones
of darkness, and the shadow of death. . . . . As for the
earth, out of it cometh bread; and under it is turned up
as it were fire. . . . . He putteth forth his hand upon
the rock; he overturneth the mountains by the roots. He
cutteth out rivers among the rocks; and His eye seeth
every precious thing. He bindeth the floods from over-
flowing; and the thing that is hid bringeth He forth to
light."

FISHERIES.

"Piscibus et stanno nusquam tam fertilis ora."
Michael Blaumpayn, or "Michael of Cornwall," circ. 1250.

The standing Cornish toast, "Fish, Tin, and Copper,"
indicates the importance of this branch of industry; yet,
although the development of many other sorts of fishing
besides that which we are about to describe will probably
ere long take place, it is with the *pilchard* fishery that
we shall chiefly now concern ourselves.

The pilchard, or gipsy herring, or "Spanish capon,"
as it used to be called (*Clupea pilchardus*), is almost
exclusively a Cornish fish, being found elsewhere only
occasionally—off the south-west shores of Devon and the
south coast of Ireland. It is like a small herring, but
the scales are much larger, and the dorsal fin is placed
much farther forward. Its flavour, when fresh caught,
or when "scrowled" (i.e. split open and dried for a day
or two in the open air) is most delicious, but it must be
eaten in the very nick of time. It is also an excellent
breakfast relish when "marinaded," or baked with
vinegar, spices, and bay leaves; it then keeps for a long
time. As an article of trade, however, the chief market
for it, when cured, is found in the towns along the
Mediterranean shores, whose inhabitants consume large
quantities. The oil pressed out of it in the process of
curing is in some request, especially for coarse out-door
painting; and the offal and brine are excellent manure.
Thus the pilchard is to the Cornishman, to some extent,
what the camel is to the Arab, or the reindeer to the
Laplander.* A good pilchard season means prosperity
and comfort for the winter; and thanksgivings for it are

* It has been said that pilchards are to Cornwall what herrings
are to Yarmouth, cotton to Manchester, pigs to Ireland, and coals
to Newcastle.

offered up in many of the churches: a bad one means starvation and misery to many a household. The habits of the pilchard, to which Mr. Couch, the author of the 'Fauna of Cornwall,' devoted considerable attention, are very curious and mysterious. It begins to make its appearance off the Cornish coast in July or August,* and retires to the deep, warm waters west of the Scilly Islands in November.

They are generally in greatest abundance towards the end of October. In that month they are sometimes so numerous that, in Milton's words, they "bank the mid sea;" the front ranks of the fish being sometimes actually forced on shore by the pressure of the enormous shoals behind them. Mr. Couch describes one shoal, or "school," as they are locally termed, which was 100 miles long.†

There are two modes employed for catching the pilchard: one by drift-nets, the other by seines. The former method is chiefly employed during the summer nights, along the south coast; and the drift-nets are so called because they are cast in a tide-way, and drift with the tide. They are about half a mile long, and 30 feet deep. The fish taken by these nets are usually smaller, but more oily than those enclosed by the seines.

The seines are more than 300 yards long, and 70 feet deep, of fine-meshed, heavy net; yet, notwithstanding this, such are the dexterity and precision with which they are handled, that they are "shot" in five minutes. The enclosure of a "school" of pilchards is one of the "sights" of Cornwall. The "huer," on the hill, whose practised eye has first descried the fish far out at sea, directs the motions of the boats by signs and gesticulations, to which the rowers in seine-boat, follower, and lurker, with their crews of about twenty men, respond with marvellous rapidity and skill. The shoal being successfully enclosed, a tuck net is employed to deposit the fish in the boats; unless, indeed, as is sometimes the case, the seine itself is dragged at high tide into some sandy cove; and the retreating waves leave behind them

---

*   "When the corn is in the shock,
           Then the fish are off the rock."
† See the Third Annual Report of the Royal Cornwall Polytechnic Society.

a wall of living silver. The exciting news of a good catch soon spreads far and wide : "fish-jowsters'"* carts throng the beach, and the pilchards are rapidly distributed round the neighbourhood, often at the rate of twelve for a penny. The great mass of the fish, however, are "bulked" and "pressed," for the foreign market. These processes are well worth seeing, for there are few such busy and merry spectacles.† Some idea of the numbers caught on exceptional occasions may be gathered from the following facts :—It is said that in 1846, seventy-five millions of pilchards‡ were caught at St. Ives in one day, worth, at 2l. per hogshead, about 60,000l.; and in 1866 there was another enormous catch at New Quay.

Sometimes, however, these capricious fish scarcely visit the Cornish coast (so that the seine is almost as speculative a business as the mine); and then there is a dull season at the principal head-quarters of the seiners— Mevagissey, Penzance, St Ives, and New Quay. It is said that the pilchard is becoming yearly more and more scarce; and that amongst the causes are the poisonous discharges from the mine adits, and the increased steam traffic.

Such is the nature of the pilchard fishery; in which not only the regular fishermen take part, but miners, townsfolk, and even strangers often join.

The regular Cornish fisherman is engaged in fishing nearly all the year round, on various parts of the English and Irish coast, from the early mackerel time in January to the disappearance of the pilchards in November; and these men have been described as " the hardiest and most adventurous " fishermen afloat.

Our notice of fishing would be incomplete without a reference to the excellent fly-fishing for trout, salmon-peal, and salmon, which may be had on most of the rivers; as, fortunately, some of the largest and best streams have not suffered from contamination by mine produce. Many of the best flies are of a local character, and should be obtained on the spot by the angler; but blue and yellow duns, red palmers, and other general favourites are pretty safe killers.

---

* Retailers.
† The pressed fish are called fumadoes (locally "fair maids").
‡ There are about 2500 pilchards in a hogshead.

ANTIQUITIES.

One remarkable feature of the Antiquities of Cornwall —"relics of the childhood of our race"—is that, for many of them, an antiquity has been claimed almost as great as that of the granite rocks and cliffs themselves, of which they are composed.

There is an abundance—we had almost written, a super-abundance—in this "land of the giants," of giants' quoits, basons, chairs, spoons, punch-bowls, wells, ladles, houses, beds, and graves; all in granite. To the latter resting-place most, if not all, of these have now been consigned by that modern Jack the Giant-killer, a more enlightened spirit of antiquarian research, which has even dared to attack the *Druids* themselves. With such *natural* objects, however (often curious and picturesque enough from their huge dimensions and fantastic forms) it is not proposed to encumber this portion of our pages; but attention should certainly be directed to other stone monuments with which Cornwall, especially the western part of it, is still most richly endowed; though vast numbers of them have been utilized by the farmer and the mason, even since the days of Borlase. The principal examples of these will be referred to in their proper places; but it will be convenient to classify them here as—

I. "*Hut circles*" (ancient British villages), which seem to bring us into closer contact with our Celtic ancestors than almost any other class of remains, and of which an excellent example is to be seen at Chysauster, near Penzance; and again, near Brown Willy mountain. As to these it should be noted that the huts in East Cornwall are generally detached from each other and are very rudely constructed, whilst farther west they usually cluster together, and are more carefully built.

II. *Cromlechs* (= bent, flat stones or slabs), as Chun Cromlech and Lanyon "Quoit" on Boswavas Moor; both near Penzance. These are huge stone sepulchral monuments; and though no doubt of British origin, have occasionally been found to contain *Roman* interments, and are perhaps the most striking and characteristic relics of the ancient inhabitants of Cornwall.

III. *Kist-Vaens* (= stone chests), also *graves*, of which

admirable examples may be found at St. Samson's
Island, Scilly; and, exposed to view, in the recently-
opened Trevelgie tumuli near Lower St. Columb Porth.
When covered with earth these objects are called *Barrows*.

IV. *Stone Circles*. As the "Nine Maidens" on St.
Breock Down, and near Penzance; and the "Hurlers"
near Liskeard. These also are probably sepulchral,
though possibly *some* of them were associated with ancient
religious and judicial ceremonies.

V. *Men-hirs* (= long stones), tall memorial stones,
sometimes single, as the Long Stone, near Penzance;
sometimes in avenues (when their original purpose is
more obscure), as at Kilmarth on the Bodmin Moors.*

VI. *Dolmens* or *Tolmens* (=holed stones), the exact
purpose of which has not been satisfactorily ascertained.
These objects have caused many interesting antiquarian
speculations, and many superstitious notions among the
common folk, who have been in the habit of dragging
wretched invalids of all ages through the orifices, in the
hope of curing the maladies of the sick persons. A
good example may be seen at Carn Galva, near Penzance.

VII. *Cliff Castles;* which abound in the Land's End
district, and are also to be found in many other points
along the coast. Secure retreats, sometimes used by the
native tribes against their invaders, or against some
hostile Cornish clan; at others, possibly, by the invaders
themselves, when they desired to secure a "base of
operations" close to the sea. The history of these relics
is not the least among the Cornish "cruces antiqua-
riorum."

VIII. *Earthwork Forts*, usually called Caers (=camps),
as at Trenail Bury, near Tintagel. These are generally
on elevated sites, and are almost innumerable through-
out the county; sometimes stonework is combined with
them, and at others (according to the locality) they are
entirely of stone, recalling the words of Tacitus—"tunc
montibus arduis si qua clementer accedi poterant in
modum valli saxa præstruit." Some of these were un-
doubtedly fortifications; whilst others, of smaller dimensions and weaker profiles, were probably only cattle

* Cromlechs, stone circles, and monoliths are erected in the
present day by the Kassias in India as sepulchral monuments.

enclosures. Castell-an-Dinas (*dinas* = fortification), near
St. Columb Major, is a fine example of mixed work.*

Such, then, may be regarded as a brief sketch of the
primæval antiquities of Cornwall; though it should be
added that many (of the earthworks especially) are,
perhaps, much less ancient than has sometimes been
ascribed to them. The *relics* found in connection with
these objects of antiquity have rarely had any very
special interest; though the gold torques and gorgets
(especially that found near Padstow, now in Her Majesty's
possession), and the gold cup found in a barrow near Liskeard, the golden amulet from Sancreed, and the curious
gold fibula found at the Lizard, may be mentioned for
the sake of their strong resemblance to ancient Irish
objects of the same class.

The early CHRISTIAN *antiquities* comprise the *Oratories*,
or small chapels (frequently associated with a Baptistery
or Holy Well), and the *Crosses* to which an allusion has
already been made under "History." Some of these
extremely interesting little churches are, in all probability, as early as the fifth century; and more than one
of them (Perranzabuloe being one of the best examples)
attest their origin by the names of Irish saints which they
bear; though the remains of most of the buildings are, of
course, now scarcely to be traced. It has been observed
by a distinguished architect and antiquarian (Mr. E. W.
Godwin) that the Cornish *Oratories* represent the ordinary type of the Cornish *Church*—viz., that they usually
exhibit no constructional distinction between nave and
chancel.

The *Crosses* (of which there is a great variety of
examples) have been beautifully illustrated by Mr. J. T.
Blight in his well-known work. A large proportion will
be found to confirm the tradition of a primitive Christianity in Cornwall.† As to their uses Wynken de Worde
in "Dives et Pauper" (A D. 1496), says—"For this reason
ben crosses by yᵉ way, that when folk passynge see yᵉ

* Many of the principal objects of this class have been
admirably described and figured by Mr. M'Lauchlan in the
'Journal of the Royal Institution of Cornwall'; and (so far as
the north-east corner of the county is concerned) by Sir John
MacLean in his laborious and exhaustive description of the
Deanery of Trigg Minor.

† See 'Archæological Journal,' vol. iv. p. 312.

croysses, they shoulde thynke on Hym that deyed on y⁰ croysse, and worshippe Hym above althyng." They were also, no doubt, sometimes erected to "guide and guard the way to the church;" and it was also occasionally the beautiful practice to leave on the crosses alms for poor wayfarers.

The Cornish crosses were once far more numerous than at present; yet it is gratifying to record that, during the last few years, many have been rescued from their servile duty as gate-posts and the like, to be re-erected in churchyard or rectory.

Churches.—It has sometimes been said that, as a rule, the Cornish churches are comparatively late and un-interesting. This is no doubt to a certain extent true; a large number of them being of the Perpendicular period, grafted on older structures; but there are many splendid exceptions. A high authority has declared that there are examples in Cornwall of "the highest and most successful times of English art." In the typical Cornish church the original cruciform plan is often modified by the addition of a long south aisle to the southern limb of the cross.*

Amongst the churches of the *Norman* period may be adduced *St. Germans* (the old Cornish cathedral), *Manaccan, St. Cleer, Tintagel, Mylor,* and *Landewednack.* Early English work is very rare: *St. Anthony,* near Falmouth, is one of the best examples. Beautiful illustrations of *Decorated* work are at *St. Austell, Lost-withiel* spire, and the large church of *St. Columb Major.* Amongst the finest specimens of *Perpendicular* work are *Launceston,* with its elaborately sculptured granite panels; and *Probus,* with its exquisite tower. Granite, though close at hand, does not seem to have come into general use till the 16th century. There are only about twenty churches in Cornwall having spires; most of them, however, have towers; and in some few instances (as at *Gwennap*) the belfry tower is at a little distance from the church. Old stained glass and encaustic tiles are rarely met with.

Of *Mediæval Military Buildings* there are very few in

* It is interesting to note how large a proportion of the churches in West Cornwall are dedicated to Irish saints; whilst for those in the north the names of Welsh saints predominate, and of Bretons in the south.

Cornwall; and they are almost all of the "*Norman*" period, as Launceston, Tintagel, Restormel, and Trematon Castles.

The *Domestic* and *Monastic* remains are not of sufficient importance to require special remark here; but such as have any particular or unusual interest will be described in their proper places.

Though not in strict chronological order, it is right here to call attention, first, to supposed traces of *Phœnician* intercourse with Cornwall, such as are exemplified by a very singular specimen of a small bronze bull, and two "astragali"—tin blocks—now deposited in the museum of the Royal Institution of Cornwall at Truro; second, to the *Roman Remains*, the scarcity of which and the reasons for it have already been noticed under "History." Traces have been found at Carhayes; at Carminow and Penrose near Helston; at St. Minver, near Padstow; Carnbrea; Hayle; Towednack; Falmouth; Carnon; and elsewhere. They are mostly coins, and therefore can hardly be considered as indicating permanent Roman settlements.

Before concluding this section, the *plain-an-guares* (= playing places), and *circular pits* with concentric ranges of steps, as at *St. Just, Perran Round*, and *Gwennap*, deserve mention; the latter are of doubtful origin, and have in modern times been turned to practical account, not only by preachers, but also by athletes. The Cornish sacred dramas, to which Norris has devoted so much learned attention, were often performed in these open-air theatres. Scawen thus describes them—"These Guirrimears, which were used at the great conventions of the people, at which they had famous interludes celebrated with great preparations, and not without show of devotion in them, solemnized in great and spacious downs of great antiquity, encompassed about with earthen banks, and some in part stone-work, of largeness to contain thousands, the shapes of which remain in many places to this day, though the use of them long since gone. . . . . They had recitations in them, poetical and divine."

COUNTY STATISTICS.

The Royal Duchy of Cornwall measures about 80 miles along its northern coast, 70 miles on its southern, and is 43 miles broad where it adjoins Devon. It has an area of 869,878 statute acres, or 1360 square miles; and its population, which is much below the average per acre of English counties, in 1871 was 362,343 persons (males, 169,706; females, 192,637). The population in 1337 was estimated at 34,960. Since the census of 1801 the population has nearly doubled, having increased by 170,062 persons, or 88 per cent.

The county comprises nine "Hundreds," and the Scilly Islands, and, for Parliamentary representation, is divided into East and West Cornwall; in the former division are the Parliamentary boroughs of Bodmin, Launceston, and Liskeard; whilst, in West Cornwall, the boroughs of Helston, Penryn and Falmouth, St. Ives, and the city of Truro, send representatives to the House of Commons.

There is one Court of Quarter Sessions for the county; and it is divided into sixteen petty-sessional divisions.

The jurisdiction of the Court of the Vice-Warden of the Stannaries extends, over the counties of Cornwall and Devon, to all companies formed to work mines of metallic minerals within the two counties; and over all transactions connected therewith. There are sixteen lieutenancy subdivisions for militia purposes, which are nearly identical with the petty-sessional divisions. The general law regulating the militia does not apply to the mines of Cornwall and Devon, the stannaries in that respect being governed by 42 Geo. III., c. 72.

POPULATION OF COUNTY, 1801 TO 1871.

Census Years.	Population.	Increase per Cent.
1801	192,281	..
1811	220,525	15
1821	261,045	18
1831	301,306	15
1841	342,159	14
1851	355,558	4
1861	369,390	4
1871	362,343	2 decrease

	£
Amount of real property assessed to the income and property tax (Schedule A.) in the year ending April, 1871	1,342,783
Gross estimated rental according to valuation lists, approved for 1871	1,344,105
Amount of ratable value	1,167,671

Amount levied for county and police rates in
   year ending Michaelmas, 1871   19,754
Amount levied for poor rates in year ending
   Lady-day, 1871   152,938

The following statistics as to the state of the surface of
the county, compiled a few years ago by Mr. Whitley, will
be found suggestive.

	Acres.
Arable and pasture lands, orchards and gardens	515,000
Waste unenclosed lands	191,500
Large enclosed crofts	60,000
Blown sand	4,350
Rivers and brooks	2,150
Hedges and ditches	18,000
Roads	10,000
Towns, houses, and farmyards	9,000
Furze-brakes and plantations	30,000
Timber and oak coppice	20,000
Total	860,000

Less than two-thirds of the whole county therefore is
under actual cultivation; of which some (especially the
soils on the trap and hornblende rocks) is as good as any
land in the kingdom, and some as sterile as the worst.

POPULATION OF PRINCIPAL TOWNS.

Towns.	Limits and Description.	Population in 1861.	Population in 1871.
Bodmin .. .. {	M.B.	4,466	4,672
	P.B.	6,381	6,758
Camborne	Town	7,208	7,757
Falmouth (Borough) ..	M.B. and L.Bd.	5,709	5,294
Hayle	L.Bd.	..	1,180
Helston .. .. .. {	M.B. .. .,	3,843	3,797
	P.B.	8,497	8,760
Launceston .. .. .. {	M.B.	2,790	2,935
	P.B.	5,140	5,468
	L.Bd.	..	3,458

POPULATION OF PRINCIPAL TOWNS—*continued.*

Town.	Limits and Description.	Population in 1861.	Population in 1871.
Liskeard	M.B.	4,689	4,700
	P.B.	6,585	6,576
Ludgvan	L.Bd.	3,480	2,960
Newquay	L.Bd.	..	1,121
Padstow	L.Bd.	..	1,991
Penryn	M.B.	3,547	3,679
Penzance	M.B. and L.Bd.	9,414	10,414
Redruth	L.Bd.	11,504	10,685
St. Austell	L.Bd.	3,825	3,803
St. Columb	L.Bd.	..	1,113
St. Ives	M.B.	7,027	6,965
	P.B.	10,353	9,992
Truro	City, M.B., P.B., and Impt.D.	11,337	11,049

"P.B." signifies Parliamentary Borough; "M.B." Municipal Borough; "L.Bd." Local Board District; "Impt.D." Improvement Commissioners' District.

MODES OF ACCESS.

On this subject the poet Wordsworth, in his remarks on Lake Scenery, seems to me to lay down a golden rule. He recommends commencing at the *lower* end or outlet of the lake; "for, by this way of approach, the traveller is gradually conducted into the most sublime recesses of the scene. As every one knows, from amenity and beauty the transition to sublimity is easy and favourable: but the reverse is not so; for, after the faculties have been elevated, they are indisposed to humbler excitement." Applying this principle to the case before us, the traveller should approach Cornwall through Plymouth, proceed westward to the Land's End and Scilly, and return along the northern shores of the county; where the climax of *natural* scenery is reached in the stupendous cliffs of

Bedruthan and Tintagel, and the less ancient work of
man culminates in "Castle Terrible," frowning down from
Launceston Hill upon the peaceful valley of the Tamar.
If the tourist should commence his acquaintance with
Cornwall at Launceston, and work westward from *that*
point, we fear that, after reaching the Land's End, he
would find a less "easy and favourable transition" to the
tamer scenery of her southern shores.

The former course is therefore recommended; and the
question next arises as to the best way of reaching
Plymouth—a town of ancient renown, and containing
many objects of interest which the traveller would do
well to inspect. Here he should, if practicable, so arrange
as to rest a night, in order that he may bring fresh eyes
and brain to the scenes and places to be described in the
following pages.

There are many ways of reaching Plymouth. First by
sea; but the route from London is somewhat long and
tedious, and many a voyager has gladly availed himself
of the opportunity presented by the steamer's putting in
at Southampton to take a fresh departure by a circuitous
land route from that port. Besides which, a shorter and
pleasanter sea trip (one which, moreover, would enable a
person to see a great deal of the coast line of CORNWALL)
might be taken on board the steamer from Plymouth to
Falmouth. The objection to this, however, is that,
unless the traveller doubles back, he misses many objects
of interest lying between the two last named places.

We are therefore disposed, unhesitatingly, to give the
palm to the rail; and recommend intending tourists to
place themselves in the luxurious rolling stock on the
broad gauge of the Great Western Railway, whose system
now embraces all the Cornish lines, including the branches
to Fowey, to Newquay, and to St. Ives.* By these means
they will most quickly reach their destination, and will
moreover enjoy the exhilarating sensations of a railway
trip along the sea beach between Exeter and Teignmouth.

The time from Paddington to Plymouth by the fast
trains, which are available to the tourist during "tourist
months" (viz. from June to October, both inclusive)

* The short mineral railway lines which branch northwards
from Liskeard to Caradon and southwards to Looe, are also in
course of acquisition by the Great Western Railway for the purpose, it is understood, of passenger traffic.

is six hours and one quarter; and a monthly return ticket may be obtained at the following rates: 1st class, 74s., 2nd class, 53s. 3d., single 3rd class, 18s. 8d. Two-monthly tickets on favourable terms are also available during the above named months. Through return tickets of the same description may also be obtained to *Penzance* —the terminus of the railway—at the following rates: 1st class, 102s. 9d., 2nd class, 73s.; but, for the reasons already mentioned, as well as on account of the numerous stations at which the tourist should stop west of the Tamar, we should advise travellers, if practicable, to rest at Plymouth, where their tickets allow them to break the journey.

PRINCIPAL WORKS UPON CORNWALL.

William of Worcester's 'Itinerary'	circ. 1478
Leland's 'Itinerary'	temp. Henry VIII.
Norden's 'Speculi Britanniæ Pars,' &c.	1584
Camden's 'Britannia'	1599
Carew's 'Survey'	1602
William Scawen (*Language*),—a fragment only—	temp. Charles II.
'Laws of the Stannaries.' By T. Pearce	1725
'Cornwall and the Isles of Scilly.' By Robert Heath	1750
Hals's 'Parochial History' (incomplete)	1750
Troutbeck's 'Scilly'	1751
'Antiquities.' By Borlase	1754
'Observations on the Scilly Isles.' By Borlase	1756
'Natural History of Cornwall.' Borlase	1758
'Mineralogia Cornubiensis.' By W. Pryce; and 'Archæologia Cornu-Britannica,' by the same	1778–1790
Shaw's 'Tour'	1789
Lipscomb's 'Journey through Cornwall'	1799
Rev. R. Polwhele's 'History of Cornwall'	1803–1816
'The Ancient Cathedral of Cornwall.' By Whitaker	1804
Lysons's 'Magna Britannia' (Cornwall)	1814
'History of Cornwall.' By Hitchins and Drew	1817
C. S. Gilbert's 'History of Cornwall'	1820
'Excursions in Cornwall.' By F. W. L. Stockdale	1824
Davies Gilbert's published 'Extracts from Hals, and the Extant Notes of Tonkin,' with Remarks of his own	1838
'The Geology of Cornwall and Devon.' By De la Beche	1839
Cyrus Redding's 'Itinerary of Cornwall'	1842
Twycross's 'Mansions of Cornwall'	1846

Dr. Oliver's 'Monasticon Diocesis Exoniensis' .. 1846
Dr. G. Smith's 'Cassiterides' 1863
Blight's 'Churches of West Cornwall' 1865
Dr. Bannister's 'Glossary of Cornish Names'.. .. 1871
Blight's 'Crosses and Antiquities of Cornwall' .. 1872
'Bibliotheca Cornubiensis.' Courtney and Boase.
    2 vols. (in course of publication) 1876–7
Lake's 'Popular History of Cornwall.' 4 vols. .. recent
Sir J. MacLean's 'History of the Deanery of Trigg
    Minor .. .. in course of publication

Those interested in the ancient Cornish language should
consult Norris's able work in 2 vols., and the Transactions
of the Philological Society. The folk-lore has been well
treated by Mr. Robert Hunt, F.R.S., in his 'Romances
and Drolls of the West of England' (1865); and, for
many places, such as Penzance, St. Just, Looe, Liskeard,
Mullyon, Cury, Gunwalloe, &c., there are interesting
monographs by various writers. There is abundant store
of information also to be found in the following books:—

'The Journals of the Royal Institution of Cornwall.'
'The Journals of the Royal Archæological Institute of Great
    Britain and Ireland.'
'The Philosophical Transactions and Magazine.'
'Transactions of the Exeter Diocesan Society.'
'Transactions of the Geological Society of Cornwall.'
        &c.   &c.   &c.

THE ITINERARY.

N.B. It has been assumed that, along the railway routes, the tourist sits looking towards the engine.

The first objects of interest to a tourist in Cornwall are so situated with reference to the Tamar, the county boundary, that, by the aid of steamboats, they may be most conveniently visited from PLYMOUTH.

The noble park of *Mount Edgcumbe*, the quaint little fishing village of *Cawsand*, *Maker Heights* and fortifications, and the *Rame Head* lie close to the Cornish shore of Plymouth Harbour; whilst, passing up *Hamoaze* under the gigantic Albert Bridge, and a few miles up the river are the Tudor mansion of *Cothele*, the rocks and woods of *Morwellham*, and the little villages of *Calstock* and *Gunnis Lake*; all well worth visiting. These, as well as trips to the *Eddystone* Lighthouse, and to *Whitsand Bay*, are so essentially the subjects of excursions from Plymouth that it has been found the most convenient course—although they all belong, geographically, to *Cornwall*—to describe them at length in the handbook of this series which treats of *South Devon*.

The CORNISH ITINERARY will therefore commence with the passage across the *Tamar* (= the big water) over the Royal Albert Bridge, one of the most audacious accomplishments even of the daring genius of Brunel. The Cornish Railway Bill received the Royal Assent in 1846; and the bridge, erected under the superintendence of Mr. Brereton, C.E. (which is 300 feet longer than the Britannia Bridge across the Menai Straits) was opened by the late Prince Consort, in 1859. It is nearly half-a-mile long, 445 feet from pier to pier, height of granite centre pier 240 feet above bed of river, height of railway above high-water mark 100 feet. The oval tubes to which the chains carrying the rails are attached (70 feet below) are 16 feet by 12 feet in transverse section, and weigh about 1200 tons each; 4000 tons of iron, 17,000 cubic yards of masonry, and 14,000 cubic yards of timber were used in the construction of the bridge. Its total cost is said to have been 230,000*l.*, and it is supposed to be able to carry about eleven times the weight of the heaviest train. Tickets for walking over the bridge are granted at the Saltash Railway Station.

SALTASH, 4½m. (formerly called Villa de Esse, Ashe, or Asheburgh) may also be reached from Plymouth and Devonport by boat, or by steam ferry. A picturesque old town, built on a steep slope, and a great nursery for sailors; the women of Saltash are celebrated for rowing in their four-oared gigs, frequently bearing away the prize from men at the various Cornish regattas. It has a mayor and corporation, whose jurisdiction extends over all the liberties of the Tamar. The church or "chapel" is dedicated to St. Nicholas, and dates from about 1225; but the tower is earlier. Edward Hyde, Earl of Clarendon, represented Saltash in 1640, and Edmond Waller, the poet, in 1685; but Saltash was disfranchised by the Reform Bill. During the Civil Wars this town was of course an important post, and was frequently taken and retaken for King or Parliament.

Leaving *Saltash*, the attention of the traveller is first arrested by the woods of *Antony* on the left, the seat of the Carews; and by *Antony Church* (early 15th century), where Richard Carew, the historian of Cornwall, is buried. *Antony House* is an uninteresting building, about 150 years old; but it contains some good portraits, especially two Holbeins.

On an eminence to the right rise the red walls of *Trematon Castle* (Trematon = ? the king's place, or the place on the great hill), one of a group of fortresses built in Norman times, either by Earl Morton, or perhaps by the Valletorts, to keep the Cornish men in order. The other castles referred to are Launceston, and Restormel, both of which are of similar design, and Tintagel. There now remain, as in Carew's time, only the "ivy-tapissed walls of the keep (on a mound 30 feet high) and base court," and the gateway. It was here that Sir Richard Greynvile the elder, with his lady and followers, was captured by treachery during the riots of 1549, as described by Carew; when "the seely gentle-women, without regard of sex or shame, were stripped from their apparel to their very smocks, and some of their fingers broken, to pluck away their rings." The position of the Castle is a strong one, and was probably occupied by a work of defence even before the Norman period. A wayside cross between the castle and the village should be noticed.

A little further on, about ¼m. from the rail, is *Ince*

Castle, now a farm house—a brick building of the 16th century—once a seat of the Killigrews. Across the *St. Germans or Lynher River*, and crowning the hill, is seen *Scraesdon Fort*, a large work constructed about twelve years since, forming with *Tregantle Fort* (about a mile and a half to the south of it) the extreme western defences of Plymouth arsenal.

St. Germans, 9½m., is one of the most ancient and interesting ecclesiastical places in Cornwall, and was the seat of the Cornish bishopric from the close of the 10th century to the early part of the 11th. The church is about five minutes' walk from the station, and the keys are kept at a cottage nearly opposite the entrance gate. It is situated in a hollow on the right of the road, and a good view of the west front (the most important feature) can only be obtained by going on a few yards to the *Port Eliot* Lodge, and so into Lord St. Germans' grounds. From this position the two western towers—one of which is octagonal, and the other square—and the richly carved Norman porch, form a striking group. The church now consists of two aisles only ; of the north aisle, with the exception of a portion which has been converted into a luxurious pew for the Port Eliot family, no remains exist. Notice especially the massive Norman columns, and the half-classic capitals of some of them, particularly of those at the north door. The east window is a very large and handsome Perpendicular one, of unusual design. There are a small portable two-handled " font " (?) and an old miserere stall at the east end of the south aisle ; and, at the west extremity, near the door, an antique carved oak panel, supporting the poor-box, on which are carved what are supposed to be the arms of the ancient see : these have been recently adopted by the Heralds' College for the arms of the Bishopric of Truro. The only other objects of particular interest are the Norman font, and an ingenious acrostic epitaph of a former incumbent of the parish, worth reading :—

```
J nditur in gelidum   G regis hujus Opilio bustu   M,
O mnibus   irriguus   L achrimis, simul urbis et agr I.
H ujus erat  vivax,   A tque   indelibile   Nome   N
A rtibus et linguia,  N ecnon   virtute   probat   I
N obis   ille  novæ   V atem (pro munere) legi      S
N aviter, et graviter, I ucundi, et  suaviter,  egi T.
E rgo   relanguenti   L icet,  eluctetur   ab   or  E
S piritus ; æternum   L ucebit   totus,   ut  aste  R.
```
E

Whitaker supposed that there was a see established here
as early as 614.* In 1358 some relics of St. Germanus were
received from his Abbey at Auxerre, and deposited in the
Priory here. The pretty little village of *St. Germans* is
another of the Cornish boroughs disfranchised by the
Reform Bill. *Port Eliot*, the seat of the Earl of St.
Germans, is on the site of the priory, and contains some
good pictures by Rembrandt, Sir Joshua Reynolds (born
at Plympton, on the east side of Plymouth Harbour),
and John Opie, R.A. (born at Harmony Cot, near St.
Agnes, Cornwall), and other artists. The St. Germans
family (of which Sir John Eliot, the celebrated opponent
of the Court party, temp. Charles I., was a member)
came from Devon in the 15th century.

MENHENIOT (= ? the old stone gate, or stone on the hill
of elders), 14¾m., is reached after passing through some
very pretty country. The village lies about a mile and
a quarter to the right, and is chiefly remarkable for
being the place where Dr. Moreman (temp. Henry VIII.)
first introduced into Cornwall the liturgy in English.
William of Wykeham is said to have once been vicar
here. On the left of the station rises Clicker Tor, an
isolated mass of serpentine, on which may be found, as
well as at the Lizard, the beautiful Cornish heath, *Erica
vagans*, which grows only on this sort of rock.

A 'bus runs between Menheniot and Looe (about 7m.),
leaving Menheniot at 7 P.M. and Looe at 8 A.M. The
tourist may, after visiting Looe, rejoin the railway at
Liskeard by walking up the pretty valley along the
canal (about 9m.), and so passing the well of St. Keyne.

[LOOE (= an inlet of water), or rather East and West
Looe—Inn, The Ship; population about 2000—are two
small towns, picturesquely situated on the banks of the
Looe River, where it meets the English Channel. West
Looe is the older but smaller place; it was formerly
called Portuan. The population of both East and West
Looe is supported almost entirely by fishing, and by
shipping granite and ore from the Caradon district. The
narrow, irregularly built, steep streets, and hanging
gardens of East Looe, where myrtles and fuchsias luxu-
riate in the open air, give a foreign aspect to the place.
A handsome but narrow old bridge, 384 feet long, of
fourteen arches, and built about A.D. 1400, connects East
and West Looe; on it was formerly a chapel to St. Anne.

* *Cf.* also Dr. Oliver's 'Monasticon.'

At the mouth of the tidal harbour is St. George's Island (also called St. Nicholas's and St. Michael's), on which once stood another chapel ; it is said persons have walked to the island at very low tides. A family called Finn, who migrated from the Mewstone, once lived on it. A battery for three guns has been constructed within the last few years, on a site a short distance to the east of the harbour mouth. Looe has been fortified one way or another for more than 270 years; for it was formerly a seaport of high repute, and in 1347 furnished twenty ships and 315 mariners for the siege of Calais. The borough was disfranchised in 1832. The church, on the site of a chapel dedicated to St. Keyne, was built in 1805. The Eddystone Lighthouse, 14 miles off, is visible from here. At the Town Hall (a new building, with some interesting modern stained glass representing incidents in the history of Looe) see the wooden porch and an ancient pillory ; the cage for scolds is gone.* Scawen, Vice-Warden of the Stannaries, and writer of an essay on the Cornish language, Horace Walpole, and Lord Palmerston have represented East Looe in Parliament. Very pleasant excursions may be made from Looe, as :

a. Up the wood-fringed river to Morval (= sea-valley), the seat of the Bullers; and to Trelawn, or Trelawny House (= the clear open place) ; the latter, an old seat of the famous race of Trelawny, has been more than once restored and enlarged; it dates from the middle of the 15th century. There is an old saying in Cornwall, that "a Godolphin was never known to want wit, a Trelawny courage, or a Granville loyalty."

The house contains amongst other noteworthy objects a portrait by Sir Godfrey Kneller, in the drawing room, of the famous Cornish Bishop of Winchester, bold Sir Jonathan Trelawny, one of the seven bishops whose committal to the Tower by James II. gave rise to the well-known Cornish ballad written by the late Rev. R. S. Hawker of Morwenstow. Mr. Hawker, however, incorporated with it the veritable old *refrain* contained in the last two lines :

> "And shall they scorn Tre, Pol, and Pen ?
> And shall Trelawny die?
> *But here's twenty thousand Cornish bold*
> *Will see the reason why.*"

---

* *Cf.* Bond's ' History of the Looes,' 1823.

E 2

The Bishop's pastoral staff is preserved at Pelynt Church.

From a place near Trelawn an ancient earthwork dyke, called the Giant's Hedge, extends for 7m. from Lerrin through Lanreath towards Lostwithiel. The history of this bank is obscure; but it is probably a divisional military line of demarcation between the Danes and Saxons. The old rhyme runs:

> "Jack the Giant had nothing to do,
> So he made a hedge from Lerrin to Looe."

b. By the coast road 5m. to *Polperro*, by *Talland* (= ? the high) Church, in which some curious wall-paintings (now gone) were discovered. Note also its tower, separate from the church; and some curious epitaphs to the Bevilles; 1m. farther on is the interesting old Cornish mansion of Killigarth (= lofty grove)—with its pious inscriptions in Greek and Latin—the seat of Sir William Beville in the 16th century.

POLPERRO (= sand port), anciently *Porthpyre*, a small, very quaint, fishing village, romantically situated in a rocky dell down which a turbulent mountain-stream splashes. The place is well worth a visit, not only on account of its picturesque situation, but also for the sake of the interesting fossils found in the cliffs, and so admirably described by the late Mr. Couch in his 'History of Polperro.' The new pier was built in 1861-2, and the harbour will accommodate vessels of 150 tons. Here, says Mr. Couch, referring to the climate, the crocus and snowdrop are seen "before they have pierced the snows of Parma." The tourist should now return to Looe.

The chief objects of interest, besides the charming scenery, in the walk along the *Canal from Looe to Liskeard*, are the Church and the Well of St. Keyne (anciently Lametton), a convenient resting-place to the pedestrian. The church, which is Early English and Decorated, lies half a mile to the left of the road, and is said to be worth a visit; but the well, mentioned by Fuller, is at any rate the more famous, through Southey's well-known ballad. Whichever, man or wife, first drinks, after marriage, of its water, will bear rule in wedded life; and the story runs that one clever woman, determined to be the "grey mare," outwitted her husband by carrying a bottle from the magic spring to church with her on the happy day.

Cyrus Redding gives a somewhat different and very amusing account of the affair.

Carew's verse is, perhaps, worth preserving:

> " The Person of that Man or Wife
> Whose Chance or Choice attains
> First of this Sacred Stream to drink,
> Thereby the Mastery gains."

St. Keyne, says Capgrave, was a holy virgin who lived *about* 490.]

The traveller passes Liskeard Railway Station about half a mile before he reaches LISKEARD (18m. from Plymouth). *Liskeard* (= the court by the castle, or the Court of Carwyd), was considered by Whitaker to have been a seat of the British kings. It is one of the half-disfranchised county boroughs; and its most illustrious representatives in Parliament appear to have been Chief Justice Coke, in 1620, and Gibbon the historian, in 1773. It was one of the four coinage towns. There is a " grammar" school and a public walk within the walls of the old castle, built probably by Richard, King of the Romans, who resided here. In 1337, "the park" contained 200 deer, but Henry VIII. disparked it. There are still some remains of an old monastic building to be seen. The church (Perpendicular, but *tower* dated 1627) is of little interest, but it contains a monument to the last of the Wadham family, the founders of Wadham College, Oxford. Liskeard is a thriving little town of nearly 5000 inhabitants, and publishes two newspapers. Webb's Hotel is a comfortable inn, and should be made head-quarters for a visit to *St. Cleer, Trethevy Cromlech, Caradon Mines, The Hurlers,* and the *Cheesewring:* a mineral railway runs close to all of these points, but at present is used only on exceptional occasions for the conveyance of passengers. The Great Western Railway is, it is believed, about to adapt the line between Looe and the Caradon district for passenger traffic.

[ST. CLEER, a straggling village 3m. north of Liskeard, situated on high ground, from which a fine view is commanded. The most interesting features of the church are the tower and the north doorway (Norman). There are, as usual in Cornwall, a holy well and a cross close by. It is said that the well has been used for "bow-sening" or ducking lunatics. Half a mile farther on is

Trethevy, or probably rather *Trevethey Cromlech* (= the
place of graves), one of the largest and best preserved
specimens in Cornwall. The inclined upper or covering stone of the grave is nearly 15 feet long by 9 feet
wide, and is supported by six others, also of granite,
about 8 feet high, the whole standing on a bed of slate
rock; "an impressive, almost a startling object to look
upon." The hole, probably artificial, in the covering
stone is now used for supporting a flag-staff on the occasion of weddings; yet it is noteworthy that similar holes
have been found in cromlechs in France, Circassia, and
India. "The other half-stone," the fragment of a granite
cross, some 9 feet high, ornamented with "Runic"
tracery, is now within easy reach; it was erected for
Dongerth, a king of Cornwall, drowned A.D. 872. The
excavations of the site, undertaken by the Exeter Diocesan Archæological Society, revealed the interesting
discovery of a crypt, of roughly tooled rock, possibly of
the Saxon period.

Another mile northwards brings us to the *Caradon
Mines*, excavated in the granite, and worked from a very
early period. Still farther northwards, and we reach

The Hurlers, possibly a "Druidic" Temple or Gorsedd,
formerly consisting of three circles of upright stones;
the largest blocks are in the middle, but many have been
removed for gate-posts, and many others now lie pros-
trate. Wilkie Collins has given an amusing account of
these stone relics on the assumption that the old legend
is true, viz. that they were once men who dared to play
at the old Cornish game of Hurling * on a Sunday.

The last mile of our by-route brings us (though the
little mineral railway still stretches somewhat farther
north to Kilmarth Tor) to

The Cheesewring, a huge, fantastic, natural pile, more
than 30 feet high, of granite slabs, nine or ten in number,
the smallest at the base; placed, amidst a chaos of other
blocks, on a hill which commands a view, in clear
weather, of the sea on both sides of the county, the
Cornish mountains of Brown Willy and Row Tor, and the
purple ranges of the Dartmoor and Exmoor hills. The first
impression is wonder that so stupendous, and, apparently,

---

* An old hurling ball is to be seen at the R.I.O. Museum at
Truro. *Cf.* Carew for a graphic account of this fine but violent
game.

so ill-balanced a mass, which has nevertheless stood unbroken the storms of centuries, should not the next moment topple over on the beholder; it is a sight which is worth a "visit to Cornwall, even if Cornwall presented nothing else to see." Somewhat similar masses of blocks, especially at Kilmarth Tor, may be seen in the neighbourhood. It is gratifying to be able to record that, in a recent lease from the Duchy, a clause was inserted to prevent quarrying within a certain distance from the Cheesewring. *Daniel Gumb's Rocks* are in the vicinity; they are noted for being the abode of a philosophically disposed miner who, nearly 150 years ago, chose this wild spot as a retreat for himself and family, in order to cultivate, at smaller cost, his taste for mathematical studies.]

Returning to Liskeard, the next station (3m.), is *Doublebois* (pr. Doubleboys), which will be found a convenient starting point for some interesting spots, viz.:

Northwards: *a.* St. Neot's Church; *b.* Dozmare Pool.

Southwards: *c.* Broadoak Common; *d.* Boconnoc House.

[*a.* ST. NEOT (anciently Neotstow and Hamstoke). Half a mile west of Doublebois Station the turnpike road from Bodmin to Liskeard crosses the Fowey River, which takes it rise at Fowey Well, in the valley on the eastern side of Brown Willy; about one hundred yards farther on, the road turns to the right, and (2¼m.) reaches St. Neot, a small village, situated on the St. Neot River, a tributary of the Fowey, and overlooked by the Tarla Rocks and an ancient encampment on the hills of Burdown. There was a college or monastery here at the time of Domesday, but no vestiges of it remain; it is supposed to have stood about a mile west of the village, near an old granite cross at "The Pound," on Gonzion Downs. The church, which was originally dedicated, it is said, to St. Guevor, or Guerrier, is the chief object of interest; it is of the Perpendicular period, and, with its remarkable windows, has been the subject of some local histories, viz. by Foster, 1786; Gorham, 1820; Hedgeland, 1830; Michell, 1833; and Grylls, 1854. The church, which bears the date of 1480, has replaced an older one; it is a large and handsome granite fabric, of nave, chancel, and two aisles, with a good carved wood roof; and, what is rare in Cornwall, a Decorated tower. The history of the wise though dwarfish St. Neot, who lived about the year 896, is given in one of the highly

interesting and effective (though roughly executed)
stained glass windows, which have made the church
famous. Some of these date from the beginning of the
15th century, and all were carefully restored about fifty
years ago. The last of the relics of the saint were removed in 1795; but the recess in which they were
ormerly placed is still to be seen in the north aisle wall;
it is inscribed "Hic (olim noti) jacuere relicta Neoti."
Notice next the fine early 14th century tower, and a
handsome old churchyard cross. *St. Neot's Well* is in a
meadow close by.

b. Dózmărĕ Pool (= the pebble-beached mere, or the mere
that ebbs and flows) lies a long six miles to the north,
amongst moors as bleak and desolate as can be found in
England. The placé derives its interest entirely from the
legends connected with it, and the superstitious awe with
which it is regarded by the Cornish labourers in the
vicinity. One of the many stories goes that the pool,
which is only from 3 to 6 feet deep, occupies the site of
the palace of one Tregeagle, an unjust steward of an old
Cornish family,* who was avaricious enough to sell his
soul, for immense possessions, to the devil. On the
expiration of the term agreed upon (100 years) Tregeagle was surprised in one of his numerous acts of rapine
and cruelty by the fiend's putting an end to the compact;
whereupon the mansion crumbled away into the surrounding waters. Tregeagle is still to be heard howling
on wintry nights, as the devil chases him with his hell-
hounds across the moors to Roche Rock hermitage, where
he finds a temporary sanctuary. But he has to return the
next day to Dozmare, to resume his never-ending task of
dipping out the pool with a limpet shell, and weaving
ropes of its rough granite sand. Another of his tortures
is to spend all night making up weary steward's accounts,
in which there is always 6*d.* wrong. The legend has
been told in some spirited lines by Penwarne, a Cornish
poet. Carew thus describes the place:

> " Dosmery Poole, amid the Moores
>   On top stands of a hill
> More than a mile about, no streams
>   It empt, or any fill."

---

* There is a room still known as " Tregeagle's " at Lord
Robartes' mansion of Lanhydroo.

Returning to *Doublebois* Station (which the tourist
should do, if only for the sake of the beautiful sylvan
views of the Glyn Valley from the railway, when he
resumes that mode of conveyance), two other interesting
places may be visited on the left (or south) of the line.
These are

c. *Broadoak Down* (= Braddoc, the place of treachery),
on which may still be seen many tumuli marking the site
of an unrecorded conflict, probably of the British period.
Here was also fought a battle between the King's and
the Parliamentary forces on the 19th of January, 1643–4,
which ended in the utter defeat of the latter by Sir Ralph
Hopton. An obelisk (half a mile north-east of Boconnoc
House), erected in 1771, to the amiable Sir Richard
Lyttleton, stands within a small entrenchment, which
marks, approximately, the position of the Royalists; the
Roundheads were drawn up on the rising ground towards
Broadoak Church. Sir Bevil Grenvil, in a letter to his
wife, dated at Liskeard, the evening of the fight, says,
" All our Cornish grandees were present at the battle."

d. *Boconnoc House* (= ? the abode of Cænoc)—where
Charles I., as well as the Parliamentarians, had, at
different times, their head-quarters — is a mansion,
embosomed in the finest woods in Cornwall, through
which runs the pretty Lerrin river; the beeches are
especially fine. The house contains a few good pictures.
The small church (which is without a tower) is Perpendicular, but of no especial interest; it is close to the
house.]

Returning again to *Doublebois Station*, unless the
tourist prefers walking to *Lostwithiel* (4m.) from *Boconnoc*
(in which case *Lanhydroc House* and *Bodmin* would be
omitted from his programme), the rail is resumed. On
the right is seen, amongst the trees, *Glyn*, formerly the
seat of a family of that name, but now of Lord Vivian,
son of the first Lord Vivian, better known to fame as Sir
Hussey Vivian, a Waterloo hero, and once Master-General
of the Ordnance. The house contains some good
pictures; amongst them are some interesting examples
by Sir Joshua, and by Opie.

Bodmin Road Station, 6m. from Doublebois, charmingly situated, is the spot from which to visit

a. *Lanhydroc House*, 1m.

b. *Bodmin*, 3½m.

Here 'buses meet the trains, and communicate (through Bodmin) with Wadebridge and Padstow, also with Camelford and Boscastle.

[*a.* LANHYDROC (= the church under the watery hill). The *Church* itself, which is (as at Boconnoc) close to the house, calls for no special remark.   The *House*, a battlemented granite mansion of the middle of the 17th century (but looking much older), is the seat of Lord Robartes, the descendant of a wealthy family of Truro merchants, and well deserves a visit ; it can be inspected when the family are away.   Here the Earl of Essex, General of the Parliamentary forces, had his head-quarters, and garrisoned the place in 1644.   The grounds are well wooded, and the house is approached by a stately avenue of old sycamores.   The building forms three sides of a quadrangle, and bears the dates 1636 and 1642 on its walls ; the gateway is interesting from its unusual form.   There are a few good old family portraits (especially in the long gallery); and the library contains many obsolete works on divinity, chiefly by Puritan writers.   Here is the Tregeagle room already mentioned.

b. There is a choice of ways for going on to *Bodmin,* viz. either by walking (about 3m. northwards), or by returning to Bodmin railway station, and going by 'bus. If the former mode be adopted, the traveller may take the road which passes the new Brigade Depôt Barracks (on the left), or follow the omnibus route, which branches off to the right on the top of the hill.   The latter will take him close to *Castle Canyke,* a British earthwork.

BODMIN (= abode of the monks, the stone house, or the dwelling under the hills) is an ancient town, the largest in Cornwall at the time of Domesday, inconveniently situated half-way between the north and south coasts, and thus at some distance from the modern lines of traffic ; it consists mainly of a long straggling street, nearly a mile in length.   From 1294 to 1868 Bodmin returned two M.P.'s ; it now sends only one ; yet, notwithstanding its antiquity, the town contains few ancient objects except the church.

Bodmin appears, in the 10th century, to have shared with St. Germans (and perhaps with other places) the honour of being the site of the Cornish see, which was finally removed from Bodmin in 990.   Its ancient name, St. Petroc's Stow, was derived from that of a Cornish saint who died about 564, and to whom other churches in

Cornwall and Devon are dedicated. The *ivory reliquary* which contained the saint's bones is one of the finest in this country, and is in the charge of the town clerk; it is probably of Asiatic make, and of the 12th or 13th century.

The Church (which Sir J. MacLean thinks is not that of the priory) is the largest in Cornwall; but only a few of the early portions now remain; these are fragments of Norman work near the western doorway, and a fine Norman font. It was nearly all rebuilt in 1469-72. The handsome south porch with its parvise chambers of two storeys should be compared with a similar one at Fowey. The tower (containing chimes) was formerly surmounted by a spire 100 feet high, which was destroyed in December 1699 by lightning: this might probably be replaced, as the tower walls are 8 feet thick at the base. The church was restored in 1819, and is now again undergoing the same process. The principal objects of interest in the interior are a pillared piscina, and the handsome altar tomb of the haughty prior, Thomas Vivian, who died in 1533. In the churchyard, east of the church, are the beautiful ivy-covered ruins of *St. Thomas's Chapel*, of the Decorated period, erected temp. Edward III., having a crypt under it: this building was at one time used as a grammar school. The other ecclesiastical remains are— at the cemetery—the relics of a chapel of the Holy Rood, built about 1501, of which only the "*Bery Tower*" now exists. Near this is an old Greek cross—one of many in the vicinity.

West of Bodmin are a few remains of *St. Lawrence's*, a leper hospital existing in the 13th century,* and there are the sites, no longer to be recognized, of some other smaller chapels.

The Priory, which stood a short distance to the southeast of the church, is said to have been founded by Athelstan in 936, for Benedictines; but it may date from even an earlier period—in fact it may have had a British origin. It was refounded in 1107-15 for Augustinian canons; and, after having fallen into scandalous disorder, was surrendered in 1538 by Prior Wandsworth. It was purchased for 100*l.* by Thomas Sternhold (Sternhold and Hopkins, the versifiers of the Psalms), and is now the residence of Colonel Gilbert.

* In 1351 no less than 1500 persons died of the plague here.

The *County Hall*, in which the Assizes and Quarter Sessions are held, was built in 1837, on the site of an important Franciscan Friary erected about the latter part of the 13th century ; the west end of the Friary is still used as a corn market.

The chief market-place is a handsome modern building of Luxulyan granite, and contains an interesting antique bell, perhaps of the 14th century ; and an old stone corn-measure, dated 1563, and inscribed

" However ye sell your mesure fyll—" *

it measures 16 gallons, or two Winchester bushels.

The County Jail, near the town, was first built in 1780, but was rebuilt in 1855–8.

The County Lunatic Asylum was commenced in 1815, but has been added to from time to time.

The monument on Beacon Hill, to General Gilbert, of Indian fame, which forms so conspicuous an object to all the country round, is 144 feet high, and an inscription records his services.

At *Castle Canyke*, 1m. from Bodmin, is a British earthwork, with two ramparts. At Tregear, 2¼m. west of Bodmin, were found, some years ago, frag-ments of Samian and other wares, two coins of Ves-pasian, and one of Trajan—interesting as being amongst the few evidences of the Romans in Cornwall. A rect-angular earthwork, assumed to be Roman, stands on the hill above.

The Royal Hotel is a large, handsome, and comfortable hostelry.

Amongst certain other old customs, the curfew bell is still rung at Bodmin at 8 P.M.]

Returning to the main route at Bodmin Road Station, in 3½m. we reach

LOSTWITHIEL (= the lofty palace, or court ; or ? the palace of Withiel), approached by a picturesque bridge of the 14th century ; an old and interesting, but small and very quiet town, prettily situated on the river *Fowey*. Lostwithiel communicates with Fowey (6m.), not only by water, but also by a mineral railway, which may

* There is a somewhat similar stone measure to be seen by the roadside from Forrabury to Barn Park ; it was probably removed from the old market-place of Boscastle.

perhaps be hereafter made available for passengers. In the latter part of the 13th century, when the Earls of Cornwall held their court here, Lostwithiel was the most important town in Cornwall; here the county meetings were held, and here only was tin to be coined. The county elections were held here till 1832, up to which time Lostwithiel returned two M.P.'s. Addison, the poet, represented it in 1704. Lostwithiel was the head-quarters of the Parliamentary troops in August 1644, who not only burnt the Stannary Records, but also did considerable injury, after their fashion, to the church, and even attempted (according to Dugdale) to destroy it by gunpowder. The *Church* (15th to 17th century) is chiefly interesting from its very strange and pretty octagonal granite spire, probably unique in England; for its singular font, for its clerestory (a very unusual feature in Cornwall), and for a group in alabaster of the flaying of St. Bartholomew—to whom the church is dedicated. It consists of a nave, with two aisles, chancel, south porch (the inner doorway of which is interesting), and western tower.

The *Duchy House*, near the church, formerly enclosed the Hall of Exchequer and other buildings, temp. Edward I.

Restormel Castle (= ? the palace of the iron rock) lies almost 1m. north of the town, and overlooks Restormel House, a seat of the Sawles, to which there is a very picturesque gate-house. The castle is situated in a commanding position, and is surrounded with foliage. The keep alone (? temp. Richard I.) remains; "a double circle of ivy-mantled walls and towers," 9 or 10 feet thick, enclosing an area 110 feet in diameter. There was a draw-bridge on the south side, and traces may still be seen of the apartments of the powerful Earls of Cornwall, who once resided here. Carew describes it as having been "a palace healthful for air, delightful for prospect, necessary for commodities, fair (in regard of those days) for building, and strong for defence;" but now, he adds, "the park is disparked, the timber rooted up, the conduit-pipes taken up, the roof made sale of, the planchings rotten, the walls fallen down, and the hewed stones of the windows, dourns, and clavels pluckt out to serve private dwellings; only there remaineth an utter defacement to complain upon this unregarded distress."

The Royal Talbot Inn is a comfortable old house; and

there is good fishing for trout, peal, and salmon in *the river*.

The line now passes along a valley in which are plentiful traces of mining operations—whilst on the hills on the right are to be seen the Fowey and the Par Consols, celebrated for the rich dividends which they once paid—and reaches (4½m.)

PAR; interesting only as being a useful harbour, and for the mining, lead-smelting, china-clay, and granite quarrying works still carried on in its neighbourhood. Par owes its importance entirely to the energy of the late Mr. J. T. Treffry of Fowey. (*St. Blazey*, a mile to the north-west, with a church dedicated to St. Blaise, the patron saint of wool-combers, is devoid of interest.) Par is the point from which the rail may be taken either north-west to *Newquay*, or south-east to *Fowey*. The latter place had better be at once taken on the downward route, and *Newquay* on the return journey.

[FOWEY (= the cave or quick river), about 4m. either by rail or by road, is an ancient and interesting disfranchised town, with excellent deep water, but narrow-mouthed harbour.* It was formerly one of the principal seaports of England; and its mariners were known as the "gallants of Fowey," for their having refused to acknowledge the supremacy of Rye and Winchelsea, two of the Cinque Ports. In the reign of Edward III. Fowey sent 47 ships and 770 mariners to the blockade of Calais—a larger number than went from any other port except Yarmouth. The "gallants," however, proving rather addicted to piracy, were disgraced, and Dartmouth seems to have taken the place of its rival port. The harbour, once defended by two square forts (one on the Fowey, the other on the Polruan side), between which, as at Portsmouth and other harbours at the same period, a chain was stretched, is now defended by a 2-gun battery at "St. Catherine's Fort." The guns of Fowey helped Charles I., who was here in 1644, to deny the harbour to the Parliament; and repulsed an attack by the Dutch in 1667. The base of an old windmill, said to have been erected in 1296, and the ruins of St. Saviour's Chapel, close to the Coast Guard station, above the transmarine

---

* The Queen landed here in 1846, and proceeded to Lostwithiel and Restormel.

suburb of Polruan (= Pool of St. Rumon or ? Roman*
port), form landmarks for the entrance.

The Church is a handsome structure, situated in a
hollow. It dates from about 1466; and its clerestory,
fine tower (100 feet high to the top of the battlements),
and south porch with parvise are interesting. It has
lately been restored at considerable cost, and contains
some Treffry monuments worth seeing.

Place House ("the glorie of Faweye"), the ancient and
historic seat of the Treffrys, overlooks the church, and is
well worth a visit, if only for the sake of the magnificent
examples of the Cornish stones used in the building and
its decorations. It also contains a few interesting portraits, and there is a fine drive to the house.

Menabilly, the seat of the memorable family of the
Rashleighs, should also be seen, especially for its remarkable collection of Cornish minerals, the chief part of
which was formed during the latter half of last century.

The by-streets of Fowey have a foreign look (and
odour sometimes), and the railway station is romantically
placed.]

Regaining the railway station at *Par*, and passing
General Carlyon's wooded seat of *Tregrehan*, curiously
situated in the disfigured landscape of the *Pembroke and
Crinnis*, and the *Charlestown United* Mines, in 4½m. we
reach

ST. AUSTELL (? St. Auxilius, or St. Austolus†), a comparatively modern town for Cornwall, which owes its
prosperity to the surrounding mines and clay-works, and
contains in itself only one object of interest to the tourist
—viz. the *Church.* It is, however, a convenient spot
from which to visit the *China-Clay Works* of St. Stephens,
Hensbarrow-Beacon, and *Carclaze Tin Mine* on the north;
and *Mevagissey* to the south. The *Church* was restored in
1870, and contains a monument on the south wall to
Samuel Drew, one of the historians of Cornwall. The
chancel and south chapel were built towards the end of
the 13th century, and the remainder during the 15th and
16th centuries. The tower is handsome, and is ornamented
with several niched statues, and with grotesque and
other carvings. There is also a curious Norman font;

* Roman coins have been discovered near Place House.
† A de Austell is said to have been Sheriff of Cornwall,
temp. Edward III.

and, over the south porch, an inscription in Cornish
which has been rendered "Ry Du," or "Give to God."
In the neighbourhood of St. Austell are some slight
remains of ecclesiastical architecture at *Mennacuddle*
Baptistery and at *Towan*.

[The most convenient arrangement for inspecting a *clay-
work* will probably be to visit one on or near the road to
Hensbarrow (3½m.), returning either by the same way or
viâ Carclaze. China clay, though latterly so important a
staple of Cornish industry—the annual produce having
at one time reached nearly 250,000*l.* worth—is a comparatively recent discovery, dating as it does from about
the middle of the last century.* Its valuable properties
were discovered by William Cookworthy, of Plymouth,
the first maker of hard or "true" porcelain in England
(unless a share in this honour may be claimed for Heylin
and Frye, at *Bow*). Its preparation now employs
thousands of hands; and the following is a brief description of the mode adopted. On the slope of a granite
hill, where there is reason to suspect, from oozing
springs, a deposit of the raw material—disintegrated
granite—a certain space is cleared of the superincumbent
turf. Streams of water are then laid on, and the surface
is disturbed by trampling and by crowbars. Sometimes the
material is collected from various stopes, and placed on
prepared wooden platforms for similar treatment. The
milk-white fluid, which is the result of this operation, is
collected by "launders" into a cistern, from which the
lighter impurities pass off, whilst the pure white creamy
matter is deposited. This is again drawn off into other
and smaller cisterns, where it dries and consolidates for
four or five months, and is then removed, in cubical
blocks of somewhat the consistency of cheese, into drying-
sheds. From these it is removed either by carts or rail
to *Charlestown* or *Pentewan* for shipment; or to *Burngullow*
for transit to the Staffordshire potteries, and elsewhere.
Such is kaolin (= the lofty ridge, the name of a hill
whence it was obtained, near King-te-chin), the sub-
stance which the Chinese so long kept a secret from the
world. The other ingredient necessary for the manu-
facture of porcelain is the Cornish growan or moor stone
(pe-tun-tse in Chinese = small, white paste) found in the
same spots, and serving to give the porcelain its hard,

---

* This trade is now in a very depressed condition, owing to
the markets being overstocked.

vitreous body. The china clay is also used for bleaching calico and paper, and for the adulteration of flour and artificial manures; and probably only one-third of what is now produced is made into porcelain.

Hensbarrow (= the ancient or King Oenus's barrow), 1034 feet high, should be ascended only if the day be fine and clear, when a splendid view may be obtained from its summit. Carew calls this hill the "Arch*b*eacon of Cornwall."

Carclaze Mine (= grey rock), about 2m. north-east of St. Austell, a huge and astonishing excavation in the earth at the junction of the granite and the killas, about a mile and a half in circumference, and 150 feet deep, is said to have been worked for tin for more than 400 years. For the last twenty-five years it has been worked for china clay, and the spot has thus been rendered doubly interesting. The view from the eastern end of the mine, between 600 and 700 feet above the sea, is also very fine.

Southwards from St. Austell a pleasant walk or drive of four or five miles may be taken down the once tin-streaming Pentowan, or Pentewan, Valley, celebrated for the interesting fossilized remains of canoes and extinct animals found fifty or sixty feet below the present surface.* The road follows nearly the line of the Pentewan china-clay railway to *Mevagissey*.

From Pentewan the tourist may proceed either by the cliffs (2m.) or by a detour of another mile through *Heligan* (= the place of willows—now rather the place of rhododendrons), to the well-wooded seat of the fine old Cornish family of the Tremaynes. Here some interesting experiments on the acclimatization of sub-tropical plants have been conducted with remarkable success.

MEVAGISSEY (= either Saints Meva and Issey, or the mill woods), anciently Lamorrack, or Laverack, a small, and sooth to say, during the fishing season, a stinking town. Here is a small harbour, where ships of 300 tons may lie alongside the pier; but Mevagissey is chiefly noted for its fisheries, mostly pilchard, in which large numbers of seines are employed. Mevagissey was fearfully ravaged by the cholera in 1849. The writer then visited it, and found, on an average, only one house in twenty occupied; the inhabitants having availed themselves of tents sup-

* See 'Archæological Journal,' vol. xxxi. p. 53.

F

plied by the Board of Ordnance to encamp on the surrounding hills. Of this scene, so novel in England, he
made a sketch, which was engraved in the 'Illustrated
London News' at the time. The church is uninteresting,
and without a tower.]

Returning to *St. Austell*, at 2¼m. is passed *Burngullow*
Station, where a "mineral railway" for china clay, &c.,
joins the main line.

At *Grampound Road* (4¾m.) a 'bus for St. Columb and
Newquay meets the afternoon train, and conveyances also
run to *Grampound*. From this point may be best visited,
if desired, the small but ancient boroughs of Grampound
(2m.), Tregony (5m.), and Probus (5m.), the latter celebrated for its church tower—the most beautiful by far in
Cornwall.

[GRAMPOUND (= great bridge or great enclosures), possibly the Roman Voluba, on the Fal, not here navigable.
In 1322 Grampound acquired the right of holding a
market. The market house (formerly a chapel), at the
western extremity of which is a cross, is in the centre of
the town. Grampound was disfranchised in 1824. There
are several earthworks, either British hill forts or perhaps
ancient cattle-enclosures, in the vicinity.

The road now runs past *Creed* church to

TREGONY (ST. JAMES) (= the dwellings on the common
near the river), sometimes supposed to be the Roman
Cenia, another small disfranchised borough on the Fal,
formerly navigable to this point. This is the smallest
parish in Cornwall. There were in early times a church
and small priory here; traces of the former existed up to
1640. *Cuby* Church is at the N.E. extremity of the town,
and contains a rude Norman font. There are also some
traces at Tregony of a castle, supposed to have been
built by one of the Pomeroy family, temp. Richard I.

From *Tregony* there is a pleasant walk of 3 or 4 miles
by *Cornelly* Church to *Probus*, whose church, rebuilt in
1852, is dedicated to the married saints Probus and
Grace. Its exquisitely proportioned tower of granite,
profusely and delicately ornamented, and 125 feet high, is
the most beautiful of the kind in Cornwall, and was built
about 1550. Remains, supposed to be those of the two
patron saints, were discovered during the restorations;
and an allusion to their names is conveyed in the prayer,
carved in wood—"Jesus hear us thy people, and send us

Grace and *Good* for ever." The church dates from about 1470, and contains the brasses of John Wulvedon and his wife, 1514.]

Grampound, Tregony, and *Probus* are somewhat difficult of access, in consequence of the distance between the stations of *Grampound Road* and *Truro.* We will therefore assume that the tourist is again at Grampound Road Station, which is 7½m. from

The City of TRURO (= three ways or streets; other suggested explanations of the name are the castle on the river, the place at the declivity of the road, &c.; but the first finds most adherents). Truro, which has returned two M.P.'s for nearly 500 years, was a coinage town, and has always been considered the principal town of Cornwall, although it has never been the *county* town, the Assizes having been held at Launceston, Lostwithiel, or Bodmin. It is prettily situated in a valley, for the most part on a tongue of land between the rivers Allen and Kenwyn, which meet at the quay-head, where vessels of 200 tons may lie. The surrounding hills are also covered with houses, and the town comprises altogether about 100 streets, lanes, and terraces. Of these the principal are Boscawen Street, Lemon Street, King Street, the High Cross, Kenwyn Street, and River Street. From Truro the rail branches off W. to Penzance and S. to Falmouth; and 'buses and vans ply to Perranzabuloe, Newquay, and other villages. The neatness and cleanliness of the town, for which it was celebrated as early as the days of James I., the width of its principal streets, and the streams of clear water which run alongside of the pavements, have an attractive appearance. Its situation, on a tidal river, and its central position have always made it a place of importance; and Truro has accordingly been selected as the site of the revived Cornish bishopric, by Letters Patent, 28th August, 1877. Several of the canonries have already been instituted, and have been named after early Cornish saints.

The town is of considerable antiquity, its first charter, obtained for it by a resident, Richard de Lucy, Chief Justice of England, temp. Stephen, dating from the middle of the twelfth century. A "castle" of the Earls of Cornwall, which formerly stood near the top of Pydar Street, probably dates from about this time. Very few traces of it have ever been discovered, and they have

F 2

been such as to indicate that the work was of no very great strength or importance.

The *Church*, now the *Pro-Cathedral*, dates from 1518; and, perhaps owing to the critical period in our religious history during which its construction was carried on, appears to have never been completed. The south front and porch, and the east end, notwithstanding the ravages of the weather on the soft Roborough stone, indicate, however, that a handsome edifice was contemplated. The monuments which once covered the north wall were destroyed during the Rebellion. It is to be hoped that now St. Mary's Church has become the Cornish Cathedral, the ugly west front and spire, erected in 1769, will be swept away, and that the venerable structure will be at length completed with due magnificence.* The interior, with its modern classic ceiling, presents no objects of very special interest; but the fine organ, by Byfield, and the monuments to Owen Phippen (1636), and to the Robartes family (1614)—now of Lanhydroc—should be noticed. There are three other churches in the town, St. John's, St. George's, and St. Paul's—all modern.

Of the more ancient ecclesiastical and domestic buildings of Truro, none now remain. Even the sites of *St. Mary's* Chapel, dedicated in 1259, and *St. George's* ("in St. Mary's Trurii"), are uncertain. The Friary of the Dominicans, founded temp. Henry III., visited by William of Worcester in 1478, was situated *near the Western Inn, in Kenwyn Street.* The earliest date at which a Prior's name has yet been traced is 1330. A seal of this Friary is preserved by the Corporation, and there is an impression of it at the Museum.

The Town Hall and Market House in Boscawen Street is a handsome granite building, erected in 1847. At its rear are the Stannary Courts, of which an account is given under the head "Mines and Mining."

The *Museum* of the Royal Institution of Cornwall (established 1818), in Pydar Street, is well worth a visit. It contains an interesting collection of Cornish fauna, antiquities, and minerals, besides many other curious objects; and the Journals of this Society are replete with information concerning the county. The Library, established

---

* It has recently been decided to remove the present edifice, which is in a dangerous condition, and to build the Cathedral on the same site.

in 1792, now removed to the Town Hall, was formerly under the same roof; and here is also preserved the hortus siccus of the Royal Cornwall Horticultural Society.

The Assembly Rooms, in the High Cross,* and also two or three of the neighbouring houses, bear witness to the period when locomotion was not so easy as it is now-a-days; and when, in the remoter parts of the country, our grandfathers had their social dissipations at home instead of in London. The building comprised a ball-room (convertible into a theatre), a card-room, &c., and, in the passages below, were formerly ranged a group of sedan-chairs, used for evening parties within the writer's memory.

The *Grammar School* (Back Street), founded temp. Edward VI., is another relic of the good old times. The building is no longer used for its original purpose, but the "foundation" continues, and the school is carried on in another part of the town. Some eminent men have been its masters; and others, who have since distinguished themselves, have been their pupils.

The Royal Cornwall Infirmary, established 1779, is another of the institutions of which Truro may be proud. It stands at the top of Calenick Street, the old road from Truro to Falmouth before Lemon Street was opened.

The last building which it seems necessary to refer to is one of which few examples remain elsewhere—the *cock-pit* in River Street—an octagonal building in a yard now occupied by a coach-builder. The site of the old coinage hall (15th century) is now occupied by the Cornish Bank.

Amongst the worthies of Truro may be cited Polwhele, one of the historians of Cornwall; Samuel Foote, the playwriter and wit (the Red Lion Hotel,† bearing the date 1671, was a residence of this family); the first Lord Vivian; Henry Martyn, the Oriental missionary and scholar; Henry Bone, R.A., the porcelain decorator and miniature painter; and the African explorers, the brothers Lander, to the memory of one of whom, Richard, a Doric column, surmounted by his statue, has been erected at the top of Lemon Street; Dr. Wolcot,

* All fairs were held at the High Cross prior to the destruction of the Castle. It is intended that the western end of the new Cathedral shall occupy part of this space.

† It seems probable that Charles II., when Prince Charles, stayed here for two or three days in 1646.

better known as "Peter Pindar," and as the earliest
patron of John Opie, R.A., resided here at the house in the
N.E. corner of the Bowling-green, now the Britannia Inn.

The best inns at Truro are the 'Red Lion' and the
'Royal.'

[Many pleasant walks may be taken round Truro.
Amongst the best may be named one of 5 or 6m. to
St. Clements, Tresilian Creek, and *Pencalenick*—thence
back by the *old* road to Truro from the E.   1m. E.
from Truro is *Penarth,* the residence of Mr. Whitley
(to whose researches in meteorology, geology, and agriculture, these pages, as well as Cornwall itself, are deeply
indebted), where a sharp turn to the right brings us, in
about another mile, to *St. Clement's.*   The church (restored 1866) is prettily situated in a hollow, and the north
transept dates from the 13th century. It contains, amongst
other monuments to the Polwhele family, one to the
memory of the historian of his native county.   Near the
gateway leading to the vicarage is an inscribed stone,
probably of the 5th century, which reads in full, "Isniocus
Vitalis filius Torrici." Turning now to the left, the road
follows the course of the heron-haunted *Tresilian* Creek *
(= the place for eels), for 1½m., when *Pencalenick* (= the
head of the moist enclosure) is reached.   The tourist
may return to Truro either by the old road indicated
above, or along the more modern turnpike.   Both are
pretty; but the former is somewhat the shorter, and
passes, on the right, Penair, late the seat of Admiral
Reynolds, and then, on the left, Lambesso, the seat of the
Foote family. Near here the road again reaches *Penarth.*]

There are two routes from Truro to Falmouth—one by
rail (11¾m.), uninteresting; except that by getting out at
Perranwell Station (about half-way) the tourist will be
enabled to visit the large and finely-timbered park of
Carclew, late the residence of Sir Charles Lemon, Bart.,
who was a distinguished patron of the arts, sciences, and
industries of Cornwall. The other route is by a small
river steamer; this is an extremely pretty trip, and will
form an agreeable change from the road and the rail,
especially if the tide be up.†   At low water passengers

* Tresilian Bridge was the scene of the surrender by Hopton
of the royal cause in Cornwall to Fairfax, in 1646.

† It is probable that the river will rapidly be choked, unless
some energetic measures be adopted to prevent it.

embark at Malpas (pronounced Mopas = ? the sea or
traffic passage). The Queen visited Truro river during
the Regatta of 1846, and Her Majesty thus describes it
in her Diary :—" beautiful—something like the Tamar,
but almost finer . . . . winding between banks entirely
wooded with stunted oaks, and full of numberless creeks.
The prettiest are King Harry's Ferry and a spot near Tregothnan . . . . Then, we went up the Truro to Malpas
. . . . from which one can see Truro, the capital of
Cornwall." The Prince and Princess of Wales also
steamed up the river in 1865.

Malpas was the scene of a sea-fight between some
French and Spanish ships, temp. Henry VIII. Here,
where the ferry crosses to *Merther* and *St. Michael Penkevil*, may generally be seen a few Norwegian barques un-
loading timber, mostly for mining purposes. On the
right is soon passed *Woodbury*, once the residence of
Henry Martyn, the pious scholar and missionary. On the
left are the beautiful woods and deer park of *Tregothnan*
(Lord Falmouth) ; and, further still to the left, hidden
amongst the trees, is *St. Michael Penkevil* Church, erected
1261, and recently restored by Street, with some interesting monuments and a remarkable oratory in its
tower. *Lamorran* (Hon. and Rev. T. Boscawen) with its
beautiful gardens, is close by. On the right, a little
farther on, is the ruined, churchless tower of old *Kea*,
formerly called *Lanege*. At *Tregothnan Boathouse* (left)
the true Fal, running down from *Tregony*, is reached ; and
soon after (left) *Tolverne Passage* (= foreigner's hole),
King Harry's Passage on the right next comes into view ;
the origin of its name is uncertain,* but tradition attri-
butes its " unde derivatur " to a visit from Henry VIII.,
who built the neighbouring castles in Falmouth Harbour,
Pendennis and *St. Mawes*, and is also said to have visited
them and *Anthony*. Next, leaving behind us on the right
the pleasant residences of *Trelissick* (= the dwelling on
the broad creek), and Porthgwidden (= the white cove),
another creek opens up, *Restronguet* (= valley with the
deep promontory), which receives the water pumped from
the *Gwennap* mines. A little further on, on the same side,
is *Mylor*, with its interesting originally Norman church

* Mr. Worth suggests the possibility of cein eru = the ridge
field.

(much altered, and lately restored), and a small Government dockyard : and, on the left, the church of *St. Just*, 13th century. We are now fairly in *Falmouth* Harbour, which the late Sir H. James, Director of the Ordnance Survey (a Cornishman), pronounced " exactly the centre of the habitable portion of the earth's surface."

FALMOUTH (= the mouth of the Fal, or Prince's River), first so called in 1660, is, notwithstanding the appearance of its name in maps dated 1500 and 1595, unmentioned by the older Cornish historians, and is a comparatively modern town, although the advantages of its magnificent and famous harbour, which receives the waters of 170 square miles of country, were known at a very early period—probably even to the Phœnicians, as evidenced by the singularly shaped block of tin dredged up at Falmouth, and now deposited in the Museum at Truro. The original name of Falmouth seems to have been Pen y cwm guic (= the head of the creek valley), corrupted into Penny come quick. Another former name for it was Smithic (= ? the smooth haven). Hotels :—The Falmouth, Green Bank, and Royal; the last named is in the centre of the town, the other two command fine views of the sea and harbour. *Arwenack House* (= a marshy place), most part of which was destroyed by fire during the Civil War, may be said to be the beginning of Falmouth. This was the seat of the celebrated old Cornish family—now extinct—of Killigrew, of " clever and courtly lineage," which produced so many wits, courtiers, diplomatists, and soldiers. An obelisk, erected in 1738, which commemorates them, stands nearly opposite the few remains of their old mansion, now used as a manor office of Lord Kimberley's. It was owing to Sir Walter Raleigh that Falmouth began to flourish, notwithstanding the opposition of the rival towns of Penryn and Truro; but the time had arrived when the considerations of security which led to those two towns being placed in their respective sites had to give way to the superior advantages of a port close to the sea. Falmouth grew most rapidly round the creek, now known as Market Strand, which once extended up " the Moor," where a good town hall has recently been built.

Falmouth has had a somewhat chequered history. It was selected as a mail packet station in 1688 ; and, in its palmy days of 1827, had 39 packets running to different parts of the globe; but in 1850 the last of the packets left for Southampton; and from the blow thus dealt Falmouth is only now beginning to recover.

Its magnificent situation, charming climate, and beautiful surrounding walks render Falmouth a highly attractive resort. It is a railway terminus, and there is always something going on in the harbour. The London-Dublin steamers call twice weekly; the Polytechnic Society, founded at the suggestion of Miss A. M. Fox, in 1833, for the encouragement of Cornish art and science, holds its annual meeting here in the autumn; * and the town contains many other excellent and charitable institutions. When it is added that in one year 3000 vessels visited the port, it is obvious that Falmouth is a gay and thriving place.

Among the many pleasant walks and drives round Falmouth, most of which command very fine views, may be mentioned one to *Budock* Church, where are some Killigrew brasses; another across the ferry to *Flushing*, and thence, by way of *Trefusis*, to *Mylor*; not to mention the numerous trips by water to different points on the shores of the harbour; as to *St. Just Church*, or to *Anthony* Lighthouse (built 1835). A steamer runs across (return ticket 6d.) to *St. Mawes* occasionally during the summer months; and other short sea voyages may sometimes be made to *Porthoustock*, *Coverack*, and *St. Keverne*.

The Docks were made about *sixteen years ago*, and the railway was opened shortly afterwards. The docks comprise tidal and floating basins, besides a gridiron, and two graving docks.

The Church, dedicated to Charles, King and Martyr, is uninteresting; it was founded by the Killigrews in 1663.

The *Swan Pool*, so called from its having been a Swannery of the Killigrew family, is a Loe Pool in miniature, but differs from it in having a subterranean outlet for its land waters. It is nowhere over 13 feet deep, and is so near to the excellent bathing place of *Gyllyngvaes* Bay†

---

* The hall contains the busts and portraits of many Cornish worthies.

† Here may be seen examples of ancient raised beaches, and a modern one of small shells. More than 250 varieties of shells have been found at Falmouth and Helford.

(= ? William's field), in front of the Falmouth Hotel, as to be worth a visit. A little further on, and the *Pennance* Chemical Works are reached; here a hoard of about 1000 Roman coins, mostly temp. Constantine I. was discovered. *Penjerrick* (= head rock) and *Tregedna*, (= ? Idno's place) residences of members of the Fox family, lie also in this direction. about 3m. south-west of Falmouth; and their lovely situation and sub-tropical gardens will delight the visitor. But the chief objects of interest at Falmouth remain to be described; viz. *Pendennis* and *St. Mawes* Castles.

Pendennis Castle (= the fortified headland, or perhaps the chief's castell) stands on a bold promontory, about 200 feet high, on the western side of the entrance to Falmouth Harbour, St. Mawes Castle co-operating with it on the eastern side. It was one of the works of defence undertaken by Henry VIII., "the father of English artillery," when he "took order" to protect our principal harbours against all invaders. It was probably held as a fortified post from the earliest times; but the present castle dates from about 1538–44, the small blockhouse near the water's edge being perhaps the first part of the work executed, and the whole being constructed (like St. Mawes Castle and most of the after fortifications on the Cornish coast) under the superintendence of Mr. Treffry, of Fowey. The enceinte is of the time of Elizabeth: Crab Quay and Half Moon Batteries date about 1795. It is an interesting example, both in general plan and details, of the military architecture of the period. A succession of the celebrated old Cornish family of Killigrews were for one hundred years its commanders; the site of the Castle belonged to them, and their seat was at Arwenack, the picturesque mansion close by, already described. The early history of Pendennis Castle is chiefly a series of complaints from the governors that they are without ordnance, and from the soldiers that they are without their pay. During the Civil War—"the war without an enemy"—Pendennis Castle played a prominent and interesting part; and was the last, except Raglan, in Monmouth, of the castles which held out for the King's cause. One of the Governors, Sir Richard Slanning, is referred to in the old Cornish distich :—

"The four wheels of Charles's wain—
    Grenville, Godolphin, Trevanion, Slanning slain."

In the summer of 1644 from Pendennis Castle the unfortunate Queen Henrietta Maria embarked for France, in a Dutch ship, sent for her by the Prince of Orange. Here too, shortly after, the Duke of Hamilton was confined, in consequence of his loyalty being suspected—a suspicion which he afterwards removed, acting, as Clarendon says, "a great part for the King." Prince Charles, afterwards Charles II., was here in February 1646—there is a room still called the King's room; and hence he sailed for Scilly on 2nd March, in order the better to escape to France.

Pendennis Castle surrendered to Fairfax,* on Sunday, 16th August, 1646, who starved out, after a five-months' siege, the gallant old John Arundel, "game to the toes," and his companions. Some of the earthworks thrown up by the garrison on the town side of the Castle are still visible, but those of the besiegers have been effaced during the last fifty years.

There is a beautiful drive, recently formed, round the promontory.

St. Mawes Castle.—So called from St. Maudit or St. Mawe, a Breton bishop (Whitaker). Leland describes St. Mawe as "a praty village or fischar town, with a piere." This Castle was also built, at a cost of about 5000*l.*, by Hen. VIII. in 1542-3, in whose honour five Latin inscriptions, said to have been composed by Leland, were cut in the walls. St. Mawes is not so large a work as Pendennis; but, from its low position and *à fleur d'eau* batteries, is a useful coadjutor in the defence of the haven. Michael Vyvyan, of Trelowarren, on whose lands St. Mawes Castle was built, was the first governor. Two barbicans were added in 1550. Eighty years after this there was a great dispute between the two castles as to which should have precedence in the matter of saluting and acknowledging vessels entering the port. This was settled by an order that Pendennis was to call to account those which anchored on the west side of the Black Rock, and St. Mawes those on the eastern side. St. Mawes surrendered to the Parliament in 1646.

The *town* of St. Mawes was "twice fyred, and the countrye thereabouts foraged" by the French, temp. Hen.

---

* The articles of surrender are given in Captain Oliver's interesting history of Pendennis and St. Mawes Castles.

VIII. It once returned two M.P.'s, but is another of
the Cornish boroughs disfranchised in 1832.

Lord Byron thus described the place in 1809:—"This
castle is garrisoned by an able-bodied person of four-
score, a widower; he has the whole command and
sole management of six most unmanageable pieces of
ordnance, admirably adapted for the destruction of Pendennis, a like tower of strength on the opposite side of
the channel. The town contains many Quakers and salt
fish; and the women (blessed be the corporation there-
for!) are flogged at the cart's tail when they pick and
steal."

The tourist will see from the map that he is now
recommended to proceed to the Lizard; and at least five
routes are open to him, viz.:—

1. Either by rail or road to *Penryn* (3m.), and thence
by 'bus *via Helston*.

2. By 'bus all the way, also *via Penryn* and *Helston*.

3. By road, through *Penryn* and *Gweek* and *Trelowarren*.

4. By the ferry across the *Helford* River and *Manaccan*.

5. Or by steamer (as before mentioned) to *Coverack*.

Most of the places of interest to be seen by routes 4
and 5 may, however, be visited from the Lizard as a
base of operations; and therefore we shall assume that
one of the first three routes is chosen, and that in about
3¼m. from Falmouth we reach

PENRYN (= the head of the river), once called Per-
marin; a small but ancient borough, which sent two
M.P.'s from the days of Queen Mary, but is now, for
representation in Parliament, united to Falmouth. Its
chief industry is the granite trade; most of the stone is
brought from the parish of Constantine, and of it,
amongst other great works, Waterloo Bridge and the
new Chatham Docks are constructed. Straw paper is
also made here. At Penryn was formerly *Glasney*
(= green ford) *College*, for thirteen Black Augustinian
Canons, founded in 1264 by Walter Bronescombe, Bishop
of Exeter; but, except the names of two or three of the
streets, no remains but a few very slight fragments of the
chapel are now to be found. No trace exists of a palace
of the bishops of Exeter, once here. *St. Gluvias* is the
parish church, prettily situated, and containing a Killigrew brass of the fifteenth century. There was also a

modern convent for nuns of Notre Dame of Namur, now closed. The corporation possess a curious loving-cup, whereby hangs a strange tale; it was the gift of Dame Jane Killigrew in 1633, the mayor having succoured her ladyship when she was "in great misery." The inn ('King's Arms') is one of the most comfortable in the county.

The road from Penryn to Helston by 'bus is (about 11m.) uninteresting; but on the high ground, about half way, in clear weather a view of the two Cornish mountains, Brown Willy and Row Tor, 40m. off, may be obtained.

[By *posting* from *Penryn* (Route 3, above) a much prettier route to the *Lizard* may be taken—viz. across the head of the Helford river at *Gweek* (=the watery village), the scene of one part of the late Charles Kingsley's novel, "Hereward the Wake"—and thence through the beautiful woods of *Trelowarren* (=the place of foxes), the seat of the Vyvyans; where is preserved, amongst other pictures, a portrait of Charles I. by Vandyke, presented to the family by Charles II. in recognition of their distinguished valour and loyalty during the Civil War. This route then leads to the Lizard over the wild *Goonhilly Downs.*]

HELSTON (= ? town on the river, or Ella's town, Helston having been a town before the Norman conquest) is interesting chiefly from its history, and as being the principal gateway into *Meneage* (=the stony district), which comprises some of the most remarkable cliff scenery in Cornwall. Inns, 'The Angel' and 'The Star.' The first charter dates from 1201, and the borough was made a coinage town temp. Edward I. For 5½ centuries Helston returned two M.P.'s; losing one by the Reform Bill of 1832. The principal street, on the slope of a hill, is wide, and at its lower end is a bowling-green once the site of a castle, which had been destroyed so early as the middle of the fifteenth century. The coinage hall is now a private house. There are good markets, which are well attended, especially on the afternoon of any Saturday which happens to be a pay-day at the neighbouring mines. The *Church* (which has lost its spire) was rebuilt in 1763. It was at Helston that a priest stabbed one of the Church commissioners during the Reformation, who, in the discharge of his duty, was

about to remove certain superstitious images, &c., from
the church—an incident which gave rise to the Arundel
rebellion, already described. At the little suburb of *St.
John's* was a hospital, founded, it is said, by a Killigrew
early in the fifteenth century. Few, if any, remains of
it exist; but there is what may be a fragment of an
ecclesiastic's tomb near the turnpike-gate at the foot of
the hill.

Helston has long been distinguished as the scene of
the Furry or Flora Dance, which used to be celebrated
here on the 8th of May with much ceremony and re-
joicing; it has now almost died out. The origin of the
name and of the custom is obscure : some connect it with
the worship of the goddess Flora ; others derive it from
$\phi\epsilon\rho\omega$, to bear or carry flowers as the dancers do on these
occasions ; others, again, from the foray which is made into
the country for bushes and garlands ; whilst Polwhele
considered it to be from the root of *feriæ* = rejoicings.
According to Jones ('Welsh Bards'), the word comes
from Ffynnu or Ffodi, signifying prosperity ; and, he
observes, it has always been a British custom to welcome
the advent of bounteous summer. The dance is performed
to a sprightly tune, said to be used also in Wales and in
Brittany ; and on Flora day in old times both doors of
all houses used to be kept open, in order that the strings
of dancers might pass through them at pleasure. The
Assembly-room, at the rear of the 'Angel Inn,' has
formerly witnessed many a ball on the night of the 8th
of May.

A pleasant excursion may be made from Helston to the
Loe Pool (3m.), *viâ Penrose ;* and this may be extended
along the Cliff road to *Pathleven* (a small fishing village
and harbour, 2m. farther on) and back by the Porthleven
Valley and turnpike-road to Helston (another 4m.).

[Loe Pool is a narrow sheet of fresh water, about one
mile long. The streams which form it are not of sufficient volume to penetrate the sandbank thrown up by the
sea ; but whenever the waters accumulate to an incon-
venient extent, a trench is cut through this bank by
permission of the lord of the manor (now J. J. Rogers,
Esq.) of Penrose, who receives, in acknowledgment of his
rights, three halfpennies in a leather purse. *Penrose* (= the
head of the moor), formerly the seat of a family of that
name, is now occupied by Mr. J. J. Rogers, late M.P. for

Helston, and a zealous Cornish antiquarian. The grounds of Penrose are celebrated for their rare and beautiful foreign trees and shrubs.]

Returning to *Helston*, a 'bus conveys the tourist to the far-famed *Lizard* (11m.). About half-way, on the right, prettily situated, are the house and grounds of *Bochym* (= the vale of weeping). The name is of great antiquity; and Robert Bochym and his brother were amongst the leaders of the Cornish rebellion in 1549. Some good greenstone celts and other ancient implements of stone were found here in 1869. On the left is another old Cornish family-seat called *Bonithon* (= the furzy abode). The road then passes over the bleak *Goonhilly* (= Hunting) *Downs*, once famous for its forest and its ponies, but now chiefly remarkable for the lovely Cornish heath (*Erica vagans*) which grows here, as in another serpentine district in Portugal, in magnificent profusion.

THE LIZARD (=the jutting headland, the gate or passage, or the high beacon).—Inns, Skewes' and Hill's; there are also a few good lodgings in Lizard Town, as the little village is called. The Lizard Town is a point from which many interesting excursions may be made ;* viz.—

a. Southward, to the Lizard Head, Housel Cove, &c.

b. Eastward, to Landewednack, Cadgwith, Poltescoe, Kennack, Crousa Downs, Coverack, and St. Keverne.

c. Westward, Caerthilian, Kynance, Rill Head, Pigeon Ogo, Mullyon, Gunwalloe, Cury.

[*a. Southward*, half-a-mile, are the two Lizard lighthouses, built in 1792 by Mr. Fonnereau, of Bochym, on the Lizard Head, the southernmost point of England, in lat. 49° 57' 39·6" N.; they are connected by a covered passage, and the electric lights may be seen at a distance of twenty miles. Notwithstanding this, it has been found necessary to add a steam fog-horn, as the crowds of shipping which constantly pass close to the Lizard render it a dangerous neighbourhood, especially in hazy weather. The first beacon appears to have been erected here in

---

* The visitor will find it much to his advantage, in many ways, to secure the services of a good local guide; and it would be impossible to obtain, either here or elsewhere, a better one than John Johns. There is also a very good account of the Lizard to be had, by the Rev. C. A. Johns, entitled, 'A Week at the Lizard.'

1619, by Sir John Killigrew. About 200 yards east is a cavity called the Lion's Den, formed suddenly, thirty years ago, by the falling in of the roof of the landward end of a cavern or "ogo." A similar phenomenon, on a larger scale and with the process still further developed, may be seen at the Devil's Frying-pan, near Cadgwith.

A pleasant walk along the cliffs eastwards leads on to Housel Cove, a pretty little bathing place, on the eastern side of which the Spanish telegraph cable may be noticed climbing the cliffs. Returning to Lizard Town, two things should be noticed—the wide hedges (the tops of which are in some places wide enough for two to walk abreast) and the deep excavations made in some of the fields for the sake of the marl, a rich natural manure. Half-a-mile east of Housel Cove may be observed the magificent natural throne of Penolver Point, and the telegraph station above it, from which news is flashed to shipowners all over England of the safe arrival of their vessels so far on their voyages; private telegrams may also be sent from here.

b. Eastward, from Lizard Point to *St. Keverne* (half the distance by cliff-paths—viz., as far as Kennack) is 11m. or 12m.; and a pedestrian would, perhaps, do well to drive back from St. Keverne; or, if the weather be *very* fine, he may go by boat to Coverack, and then return on foot.

LANDEWEDNACK (= the white-roofed church, or church of St. Wednoc), ⅜m., in a sheltered situation, has a good Norman south doorway with groined porch, a Perpendicular tower of large granite and serpentine blocks, and a hagioscope and window, possibly constructed for the use of lepers. Here, it is said, the last sermon in the Cornish language was preached in 1678. Another ¼m. and the fish-cellar and landing-place of *Perranvose* are reached; here the tourist will embark if he goes eastward by water. The cliff-path, however, commands beautiful views, though it does not enable the magnificent caverns—Dollah and Raven's Ogos—to be inspected; however, the celebrated Balk serpentine quarry and the Devil's Frying-pan (from above) will be seen by this route.

CADGWITH (= ? scedgewith = privet), a characteristic little fishing village, with small inn, is 2½m. from Lizard Town. In another mile along the edge of magnificent cliffs, against which many a ship has been dashed to pieces, are the wooded valley, small trout stream, and serpentine works of Poltescoe (= ? the pool below the wood); 1m. farther on is Kennack Cove, a long sandy beach, where may be found, on the low cliffs, asbestos and mountain leather, and in the marsh, at its eastern extremity, one or two very rare plants. It may here be noted that the wild asparagus and several other botanical curiosities are met with in this district. Had Kennack been within 100m. of London, what a popular resort it would have become!

The road now leads, for 5 or 6m., over Crousa Downs (= the cross), a chaotic mass of diallage rocks, to *St. Keverne*, one of the most fertile parishes in Cornwall—*Coverack Cove*, a pretty little fishing village, lying 1m. to the right. At the comfortable little inn of St. Keverne was born Charles Incledon, a celebrated barytone singer; his father's name, "Michael Incledon," may be seen carved in stone at the back door. (Incledon = the angel of the hill.) The *church* (with its ribbed spire and fine bell), one of the largest in Cornwall, is chiefly Perpendicular, but there is some much earlier work in the north aisle; the carved ends of the pews, and an acrostic epitaph should also be noticed.

c. Westward (this route also, in very fair weather, may be taken by boat).—A path leads from Lizard Point to Pistill Cove, ½m. (= the shoot of water), and then westward to *Caerthilian*, suitable for bathing at low water. 1m. farther is *Pentreath* Beach, where, on moonlight nights at low-water spring tides, good sport may be had on the sands "launcing." The launce is a delicate little fish, not unlike the smelt in flavour; and the sport of catching it, with long iron hooks fixed to wooden handles and dragged through the sand, is at once novel and exciting.

At length is reached, 2½m. from Lizard Point by this route, a spot whose rare beauty has been extolled perhaps more highly than that of any scene in Cornwall—*Kynans* (= the brook of the dog). The best time for visiting this spot (where clean, humble lodgings at either of two small cottages may be obtained) is at low tide, on a bright summer day, after stormy weather. Its soft, yellow, sandy beach, its emerald waves, deep rock-pools, and its gorgeous serpentine cliffs of motley colours (green, purple, crimson, and black) are then of astonishing beauty. The storms of winter wash away the sand, and the beach is then seen strewn with boulders of serpentine,

G

diallage, and hornblende. The tall columnar rock is called the *Steeple;* on the land side of it are caverns known as the *Drawing Room* and the *Kitchen,* communicating with each other.

Asparagus Island, on which wild asparagus formerly grew,* is on the seaward side. It is pierced with a hole which, at certain states of the tide, is the cause of strange phenomena ; a retreating wave causes a piece of paper to be violently sucked in—this is the " Post Office ;" whilst the rising surge is shot out in a jet of dazzling foam, which, under favourable conditions, forms an exquisite iris—this is known as the " Bellows." Outside *Asparagus Island* (which can be climbed with some little danger and difficulty), and separated from it by a hideous chasm, " *the Devil's Throat,*" where more than one fatal accident has occurred, is the *Gull Rock.*

The tourist will be tempted to linger at least three or four hours at *Kynans;* and then ½m. of rugged ascent, and the grand headland known as *Rill Point* is reached, from which most extensive views of the Land's End district and the Lizard Head may be obtained. Another ½m., and we come in sight of a jagged ridge stretching out into the sea, and called the *Horse* ; ½m. beyond it is perhaps the most terribly magnificent cliff in Cornwall—*Pigeon,* or rather *Poethon Ogo* (= the boiling cave), a sheer wall of rock 250 feet high, with a cave at its base. The colouring of this precipice, under certain conditions of light, is superb. Another ¼m., and *Gue Graze* (= the winding valley) is reached ; it is otherwise known as *Soapy Cove,* from its cliffs having been worked, at the end of the last century, for steatite or soap-rock (a stone of unctuous touch), by Flight of Worcester, for making porcelain.

The cliffs may now for a while be forsaken; and the tourist may proceed through *Pradannack* village, with its interesting stone cross, to *Mullyon.*

MULLYON (= St. Melianus; or ? the cold, bare place), about 8m. from Lizard Town, along the cliffs, should on no account be omitted by the visitor to the Lizard, who would do well to provide himself with a charming little volume, descriptive of the parish, by the vicar, Rev. E. G. Harvey. The iron-bound coast has seen many a wreck; twenty-three are known to have occurred between

* It is still to be found in this vicinity.

1809 and 1873, of all of which Mr. H. gives painfully interesting accounts. Amongst other natural curiosities * here may be mentioned native copper, of which a lump of 15 cwt. was once discovered. The serpentine caverns at Mullyon Cove, and the Cove itself, are also very picturesque. Dean Alford wrote that " it is vast in extent, and unites in itself almost all the characteristics of Cornish coast scenery ;"—but it is essential that it should be visited at low tide. The church, restored in 1870, is a late 15th century building, standing on the site (as in the case of so many others in Cornwall) of an earlier building (probably, in this case, of the 12th century). It is dedicated to that saint who also gave his name to St. Malo in Brittany. Indeed, it is curious to notice how many of the churches along the Mount's Bay shores are dedicated to persons who afterwards retired to Brittany. The admirably-carved benches, amongst the best in Cornwall, are its most noteworthy feature, and will repay a careful examination. But our description of Mullyon would be unpardonably incomplete without a special reference to the " Old Inn," kept by Mary Mundy. Without any approach to pretentiousness, it is one of the most comfortable that can be met with, and well merits the encomiums bestowed upon it by many of its visitors. Some of these are remarkably well indited ; but two must suffice here :—

" Hospitium mundus tenet hospes munda magistra ;
Munditiâ floret sic vetus illa domus ; "

and the two concluding verses of a capital little *jeu d'esprit* written in 1872, by Professor Blackie, which he entitled

" LAUDES HOSPITII VETERIS, ET DOMINÆ MARIÆ MUNDÆ.

*　　　*　　　*　　　*　　　*

" And I advise you all to hold
By the well-tried things that are good and *old*,
Like this snug house of Mundy ;
The good Old Church, and the good Old Inn,
And the good old way to depart from sin,
By going to church on Sunday.

---

* *Genista pilosa*, a hairy green weed, has been noticed at Gue Graze.

> " And if there be on Cornish cliffs,
>   To swell his lungs with breezy whiffs,
>   Who can spare but only ONE day,
>   Let him spend it here; and understand
>   That the brightest thing in Cornish land
>   Is the face of Miss Mary Mundy."

A further very interesting feature of Mullyon is the poetic character of the names of many of its hills and vales; suggestive to an old Cornishman, Mr. Harvey supposes, of some such thoughts as these:—

" Let us away by $\left\{ \begin{array}{c} \text{Le Flouder} \\ \text{the water springs} \end{array} \right\}$ to $\left\{ \begin{array}{c} \text{Polurrian,} \\ \text{the sea-birds' home,} \end{array} \right\}$

on past $\left\{ \begin{array}{c} \text{Carrag lûz,} \\ \text{the hoary rock,} \end{array} \right\}$ $\left\{ \begin{array}{c} \text{Porth Mellin,} \\ \text{the mill cove,} \end{array} \right\}$ and the $\left\{ \begin{array}{c} \text{Vro,} \\ \text{brow,} \end{array} \right\}$

to $\left\{ \begin{array}{c} \text{Creeg Morgan.} \\ \text{the stony hillocks by the sea.} \end{array} \right\}$ "

From Mullyon (1½m.), past *Poljew Cove* (= the black or bream pool), is *Gunwalloe.*

GUNWALLOE, or Winwaloe, the Victorious Wallo, a Breton saint, to whom Landewednack Church, and also two or three Welsh churches, are dedicated, was a pupil of St. Budoc's, and died A.D. 529.

The *Church*, said to be the votive offering of some shipwrecked mariner, nestles under a cliff, and is washed by the waves. The tower is separated by 14 feet from the church.* The present east and west walls are probably of the 14th century, and the remainder of the 15th century. It has a good carved open roof, and there are panelled paintings on the screen. An old Norman font-bowl may be noticed under the west window, bearing the ancient mark of the Trinity, ⋀. The three bells bear curious Latin inscriptions. The church was restored 1869-71, at a cost of £550. The cross, which once lay in the stream, was removed to Penrose for safety, and is now placed at the S.E. angle of the chancel wall. The parish records, as might be expected from the nature of the coast, teem with entries of the burials of ship-

---

* Separate bell-towers are also at Feock, Mylor, Gwennap, and Lamorran.

wrecked persons The epitaph of Joseph Dale, who was drowned in April 1808, while endeavouring to rescue one of the crew of a ship wrecked at the Loe Bar, quaintly ends,—

> " But tho' his mortal part be dead,
> His spirit lives above;
> *Where he may bathe from dangers free*
> *In seas of heavenly love."*

Wonderful instances of skill and daring in attempts to rescue shipwrecked crews are recorded in Mr. Cumming's ' Cury and Gunwalloe' and Mr. Harvey's ' Mullyon.' One celebrated wreck was of a ship laden with Spanish dollars, nearly 100 years ago. Only a few specimens of her valuable cargo have ever been recovered, notwithstanding many attempts (one of which is now before the public under the name of "The Dollar Recovery Company ").

About 1m. inland is *Cury* (and here the pedestrian would gladly meet with a vehicle to take him back to Lizard Town, a drive of about 8m.). Cury is so called from St. Corantyn, the first Cornish apostle of any note. He was a bishop of Cornwall, and a confessor, and died about A.D. 401. The *church* consists of a chancel and nave, 14th century; a north aisle, 15th century; and the south or Bochym aisle. There is a handsome Norman doorway, and the curious carved roof represents (*inter alia*) Cornish miners at work. There is also a hagioscope, as is often the case in the Lizard district, which has probably helped to give currency to the tradition that leprosy or elephantiasis was once prevalent here. Fragments of some curious alabaster carvings were discovered during the restoration of the church in 1874. Cury Cross has been supposed to date from the first century of our era.]

The tourist is recommended to return from Lizard Town to *Helston* by 'bus, in time to catch the corresponding 'bus to Penzance.

Leaving Helston, 3½m. right is *Breage* (so called after St. Breaca, an Irish saint) church and village, through which the old road used to pass. At the church the principal objects of interest are helmets and tombs of the celebrated but now extinct Cornish family,

Godolphin* (= ? a little valley of springs), whose seat, of
the same name, lay 2m. to the N., and of which some
remains exist. *Tregonan Hill* (=the place on the downs),
595 feet high, now comes well into view on the same side
of the road, standing in the midst of a rich mining
district. It was from Tregonan Hill that Cookworthy
procured the materials for the Plymouth hard-paste
porcelain. 6m. from *Helston* and ½m. to left is *Pengers-
wick Castle*, a Tudor residence, containing some quaint
carvings and inscriptions. 2¼m. farther on and ½m. to
left is *Perranuthno Church* (= Perran on the high, bare
place). In a cave near, tradition says that Trevilian,
the only man who escaped when *Lyonesse* (see section
on Physical Geography) was submerged, found shelter.

In 10m. is reached *Marazion* (= markets, marha-
sion), alias *Market Jew*, probably the older name (=
markets, marchadyou): the "little market" has also
been suggested as the meaning of the name. It is called
Marchadyou in a charter of 1257, and Marghasiewe in
another of 1595. Camden calls the place Merkin. It
appears to have no connection with the word *Jew*; and, in
fact, most of the stories of the Jew miners and smelters
of Cornwall seem to have taken their rise in an etymological blunder.† Probably one of the most ancient
markets in the world, having been a trading-place for
tin in the days of the Phœnicians, Marazion is now a
small and uninteresting borough, but possesses some
curious relics in the charge of the corporation. Once
the post-town for Penzance, it dwindled into its present
condition from the time when ecclesiastical pilgrims
ceased to visit the shrine on St. Michael's Mount; nor
have the numberless tourist pilgrims of the present
time (in consequence of the propinquity of *Penzance*)
hitherto been able to re-establish its ancient importance.
Marazion was burnt by the French in 1513–14, though
the townspeople afterwards drove them off; and again
in 1549, during the Arundel rebellion already referred to.
In front of Marazion, ¼m. from the strand, rises "the
guarded mount," as far-famed in England as its counter-

---

* A member of this family is said to have invented mine-
stamps in the 16th century.

† *Cf.* Professor Max Müller's elaborate essay, "Are there
Jews in Cornwall?"

part, Mont St. Michel, in Normandy. At low tide the tourist may walk across over a rough causeway; but at high water a boat is indispensable, for St. Michael's Mount, as Carew says, is "both land and island twice a day." * It consists of an isolated rugged pyramid of granite, intermixed with slate, greenstone, and veins of quartz; presenting many difficult geological problems. It is about a mile in circumference at the base, and 230 feet high at the chapel platform. Visitors are admitted to the interior in the absence of the St. Aubyn family, to whom St. Michael's Mount belongs. Six Sir John St. Aubyns successively inherited it. The Chapel and the Hall (known as the Chevy Chase room, from its frieze) are both mostly of the Perpendicular period, though the former has been much tampered with, and the latter bears a date 1660. These two parts of the building and the entrance itself are the portions most worthy of examination. A few steps below the floor of the chapel is a recess called the dungeon; near it a very narrow winding stair leads to the tower (15th century) roof. At one angle of its platform are the remains of a stone cresset called St. Michael's Chair, or "Kader Mighel," which possesses similar virtues to the well of St. Keyne, who, curiously enough, is said to have once paid a visit here. Even some *ladies* are foolish enough to get into this dangerous seat. The drawing-rooms are modern, on the site of the conventual buildings, and contain two portraits said to be by Opie, one of them of the Dolly Pentreath, *alias* Jeffery, who is referred to in the section on "Ancient Cornish Language."

St. Michael's Mount's legendary history commences as early as the 5th century. Edward the Confessor granted the Priory by charter, in the middle of the 11th century, to some monks, and it was subsequently annexed to Mont St. Michel. From a very early period it was a fortified as well as a religious dwelling. It was held for King John for a short time; was seized by stratagem, and defended by the Earl of Oxford for Henry VI. against Edward IV.,

---

* Mr. Edmonds considers that this causeway is not available for so long a period during each day as it formerly was. At spring tides, high water, it is about 12 feet below sea-level, and at low water about 6 feet above it; but occasionally, in rough weather and neap tides, one cannot walk across for two or three days together.

but ultimately surrendered. Edward granted it to the Abbey of Syon, to which it remained attached till the Dissolution. Edward VI. dispossessed the Arundel rebels of it; and it surrendered to its victorious Parliamentary besiegers in the time of the Civil War. It seems now to be generally agreed that this is the *Ictis* of Diodorus Siculus. The little fishing village at the foot of St. Michael's Mount has a few picturesque houses, and the harbour accommodates vessels of 500 tons. The first pier or quay seems to have been erected by one of the monks, temp. Hen. VI.; it was rebuilt by the St. Aubyn family in 1726-7. It should, perhaps, be noted here that the name of "the hoar rock in the wood," formerly applied in error to St. Michael's Mount by the older Cornish historians, appears to have rather belonged to its Normandy counterpart. A learned essay on the subject has been written by Professor Max Muller, entitled "The Insulation of St. Michael's Mount."

The tourist may now proceed, as time and opportunity serve, either by rail, by 'bus, by boat, or on foot along the beach (the site of a celebrated submarine forest) to *Penzance.*

PENZANCE (= the holy headland; and not the holy *head,* as is sometimes assumed from the head of St. John the Baptist, in a charger, having been chosen in the 17th century as the town arms) is 328m. by rail, or eleven hours from London. It is the "basis of operations" for the *Land's End* district. Its early name is said to have been *Buriton* (= Castle Town); and, although there may be but slight evidence of this, yet it may be observed that there is a "Barbican" Street near the Quay. There is no doubt that, temp. Edward III. (1332, Mr. Courtney says), Penzance was granted a market and a fair. Another dim glance at Penzance in ancient times is afforded by the tradition that, towards the close of the 13th century, there was a chapel to St. Anthony near the Pier headland, on the west side of Barbican Street, and that there was another chapel here (the site of which is unknown) dedicated to St. Gabriel and St. Raphael, and licensed in 1429. The chapel of St. Mary was licensed in 1397.—The history of Penzance during the next century is a blank. Early in the 16th we find it a busy trading port, obtaining a charter from Henry VIII. in 1512; and, in the middle of that century, we

find Sir Walter Raleigh here, smoking the first pipe of
tobacco ever consumed in England. In July, 1595, an
invasion was made by the Spaniards (said to be the only
Spaniards who ever landed as enemies on English soil)
when Penzance, *Mousehole*, and *Newlyn* were all more or
less burnt by the marauders: they were, however, at
last boldly met by the natives, when they had recovered
their first surprise, and the Dons were driven back to
their galleys. In 1615, Penzance received a charter from
James I. Fairfax sacked the place in 1646, in consequence of its having too loyally harboured the troopers
of the Lords Goring and Hopton. Two years later the
sympathy of Penzance for the Royal cause was again
manifested by a rising, which was however speedily
suppressed. Such devoted loyalty could not pass un-
rewarded; and Penzance was accordingly, in 1663, made
the fifth and last of the coinage towns of Cornwall.* It
appears to have subsequently somewhat fallen from its
higher estate; as, in 1780, Dr. Davy (brother of Sir
Humphry) writes that his mother told him she remembered the time when there was only one cart and one
carpet in the town. Things have very much improved
since then; and Penzance, the westernmost town of
England, has become a railway terminus, and one of the
largest and most important towns of Cornwall, if not,
indeed, the first in size.

St. Mary's Church, which had long remained in a
ruinous state after the Spanish raid, was repaired in 1665,
and enlarged in 1728.† It was rebuilt of granite on the
site of the latter structure about forty years ago, and is
spacious, but of no particular interest. The churchyard contains a fragment of an old cross supposed to
have come from St. Anthony's chapel, and the tombs of
many a stranger invalid, whose deep-seated pulmonary
complaints not even the marvellous, Mediterranean climate of the Mount's Bay could save. The beautiful
little Early English Church of *St. Paul*, built in 1843
by one of the highly esteemed family of Batten of
Penzance, is a gem well worth inspecting. The general

* The other four were Launceston, Lostwithiel, Truro, and
Helston; but all ceased to be coinage towns on the abolition of
the tin duties in 1838.

† There is an alms-box dated 1612, and the old font was inscribed 1668.

effect of the interior is remarkably solemn; and the stained glass and the pulpit are worthy of especial notice.

The *Pier*, which is the largest in Cornwall, was built or rather rebuilt, about 130 years ago; but the north arm of the harbour was not constructed till 1845. This makes the harbour, which is tidal, very safe and commodious; and it often presents a busy and picturesque scene. St. Michael's Mount, 3m. off, and the strange plateau of the Lizard District looming in the grey distance (the Head is 20m. away) materially add to the beauty of the view. It is understood that the formation of Docks is contemplated. Here it should be mentioned that a fine esplanade has been constructed westward of the Pier, which forms a popular promenade; along it are two good hotels, and several lodging houses. There is also a *natural* esplanade of sandhills on the opposite side of Penzance, stretching eastwardly from the railway station.

The public buildings of Penzance are very creditable. The Town Hall and market house, whose dome is conspicuous from all the surrounding country, stands in the centre of the town, and contains also the Post Office and formerly a very interesting though small Museum of Antiquities, &c. Amongst the most noteworthy objects in the latter are carefully executed models, to scale, of the principal ancient stone monuments of the neighbourhood. The building was erected on the site of an older market place, in 1837. Let into the wall at its eastern end is an antique cross, probably of the 6th century, the inscription on which (now hidden) is, "Hic procumbunt corpora piorum;" and a little in advance of the western portico, overlooking the fish market, is the statue of the Inventor of the Miner's Safety Lamp, that illustrious chemist, a native of Penzance, Sir Humphry Davy. Penzance may well be proud of such a son; and also to count upon her roll of worthies of the last century the gallant Admiral, Lord Exmouth;* and one of the historians of his native county, Davies Gilbert, P.R.S. In 1867, some fine new Public Rooms were completed: they contain the Municipal Offices, the spacious St. John's Hall, &c., the excellent library and collections of

* *Cf.* E. Osler's 'Life of Exmouth.'

the Royal Cornwall Geological Society, established in 1814—a Public Library, and a Natural History Museum, &c. Mr. Carne's celebrated collection of minerals, in New Road, should also be inspected by all who care to be amazed at the wonderful and beautiful objects contained in the depths of the Cornish mines. Penzance is further well supplied with charitable and other institutions.

As showing the remarkable climate and fertility of the soil of this part of England, it may be mentioned that, in sheltered spots, potatoes have been dug at Christmas; ripe *kidney* potatoes on the 1st of April; and that strawberries have been sold at 6*d*. per gallon. On one New Year's day, the following were amongst the flowers in full bloom in the open air: geraniums, hollyhocks, sweetpeas, mignonette, carnations, magnolias, fuchsias, and roses of all kinds! Under such circumstances it will not be wondered at that horticulture for the London market is one of the staple industries.

The defences of Penzance consist of a modern 2-gun battery, which overlooks the railway station. There is also a battery site near the pier-head, and another at *Gwavas*, about 2m. S. of Penzance.

The walks in the immediate neighbourhood of Penzance are justly celebrated; but the tourist will need no guide to them, as he can scarcely go wrong in any direction. The hotels, amongst which the best are 'The Queen's' and 'Mount's Bay House' (on the Esplanade), 'The Union' (in the centre of the town), and 'The Western' (pleasantly and quietly situated), are generally approved.*

THE LAND'S END DISTRICT is full of objects of interest; and its granite cliff scenery is amongst the finest in Cornwall. During the season four-horse vehicles convey tourists to the *Logan Rock, Land's End*, and back, for 3*s*. Omnibuses also ply between *Penzance* and *St. Just*, which will be found convenient for more than one of the following excursions—even to those who are good pedestrians. Perhaps the best way of seeing many of the principal points would be to subdivide the district in the following manner :—

    a. Newlyn, St. Paul, Mousehole, Lamorna, Rosemo-

* There is a useful little 'Official Guide to Penzance.'

dress, Dawns-maen, the Pipers, British Cave, Boleit, Tre-woof. (Sleep at *Penzance.*)

b. Lower and Higher Drift, Boscawen-un, Circle of the Nine Maidens, Buryan, Logan Rock and Cliff Castle, Sennen, Land's End. (Sleep at *Land's End.*)

c. Maen Castle, Whitesand Bay, Cape Cornwall, Ke-nidzhek Castle, St. Just, Botallack. (Sleep at *St. Just.*)

d. Tregeseal Circles, Carn Kenidzhek, Chun or Chy-woon Cromlech and Castle, Men-an-tol, Men-scryfa, Nine Maidens, Lanyon Cromlech, Madron Church and Well. (Sleep at *Penzance.*)

a. This excursion (a round of about 11m.) should be made on foot. Leaving Penzance, and passing the celebrated subterranean *Wherry Mine*, 1m. S.W. from Penzance, is the little fishing village of *Newlyn* (= the open lake), to whose history reference has already been made. Another mile brings us to *St. Paul* or (as it should rather be written, according to some authorities) *St. Pol*—the name of the patron saint being sometimes considered the same as that of St. Pol de Leon, in Brittany; whilst others contend that the church was dedicated to St. Paulinus, first Arch-bishop of York. From this part there are fine views of Mount's Bay. The church, Perpendicular, contains a tablet to one of the Godolphins, and an old epitaph, in Cornish; and here also is a monument to the possibly too far-famed Dolly Pentreath. At the foot of the hill, to the S., lies picturesque but odoriferous *Mousehole** (= either the Maiden's River or the Sheep Moor), whose ancient name was Port Enys (= the Island Port). Notice the old resi-dence with a porch, now the 'Keigwin Arms.' A walk of two miles farther along the edge of the cliff and once beautiful *Lamorna Cove* is reached (= Morvah = near the sea). Here are granite quarries, exhibiting numerous varieties of this rock.

Ascending the opposite hill, in a westerly direction, we reach, in one mile, Rosemodress (= the heath with a circle), the circle being the nineteen stones called the Dawns Maen, or dancing maidens—damsels who were turned into stone for dancing on a Sunday. Close at hand are two taller menhirs, known as "The Pipers," who

* A right of quayage was granted to Mousehole by Richard II. in 1393.

appear to have participated in the punishment as well as
in the festivity. There are several other stone circles
in this part of Cornwall, many of which are said to
have originally consisted of nineteen stones (a number
generally abbreviated by the inhabitants into nine),
whence the theory that they were dedicated to Apollo,
"who is supposed to have visited Britain once every
nineteen years." At *Boleit*—pronounced Boleigh—(= the
place of slaughter), it is said that the Britons made
their last stand against the Saxons. Within a stone's
throw is an ancient British Ogo, or Fogo (= cave).
Descending into the valley, and crossing the stream at
its foot, the old mansion of *Trewoof* (= the place of
blackbirds), connected by a subterranean passage with
an old entrenchment, is reached in a few minutes; and
the tourist may now either descend the Lamorna Valley
and return to Penzance by the route he has already tra-
versed, or make for *Newlyn*, 3½m., through Chywoon
(= place of the town).

b. This excursion may be most conveniently made by
one of the four-horse conveyances already mentioned.
Again touching Newlyn on our way, we pass through
the wooded valley of Trereiffe (pr. Treeve) and over Bur-
yas Bridge. About 3m. from Penzance are Lower and
Higher Driff (= dwellings), with their ancient monumental
stones. Crossing three steep-sided valleys,* each with
its small stream, we reach, 6m. from Penzance, *St.
Buryan*, where a short halt is generally made. The
little village of St. Buryan (so called after Buriana, an
Irish saint) is a place of considerable historic interest,
and is said to have been the site of a college founded by
Athelstane to commemorate his conquest of Cornwall.
The supposed site is ½m. E. of the village, and is called
Sanctuary Hill; but no traces of the buildings remain,
though they are said to have been in existence some
years ago. The Cross, with its sculptured figure,
and five bosses suggestive of the five wounds of our
Saviour—in the open space in front of the churchyard—
is a curious example. The fine Church, 520 feet above
the sea, has been recently restored. It is mostly temp.
Henry VII., but has much older portions. The quaint

---

* 1m. north up the third of these valleys is the celebrated
stone circle of the "Nine Maidens" of *Boscawen un.*

carvings should be noticed; also the epitaph of a Levelis of Trewoofe. The tower is the highest in Cornwall, except that of Probus; and from its summit a magnificent view may be obtained. It is one of the few churches in Cornwall where a few fragments of the original stalls are now to be found. Noye, Attorney-General to Charles I., was born at Pendrea, near here, in 1577. Crossing two or three more valleys, in another 2m. we reach *Trereen*, pronounced Treen (= the place on the headland), a small, quaintly-situated hamlet, where passengers dismount for a walk of ⅜m. across fields to *The Logan Rock*. There are several such rocks amongst the granite tors of Cornwall and Devon, but this is the most remarkable from its size and situation. There is some little difficulty in climbing up to it; and the huge mass, weighing over 70 tons, only *logs* or rocks now very slightly, it having been wantonly displaced some fifty years ago. It was indifferently replaced by the culprit a few months afterwards.* The headland on which it stands, *Trereen Dinas* (dinas = fortification) is one of the best examples of a cliff-castle in Cornwall. Notice its three semicircular embankments. The fantastic shapes of some of the granite rocks in the vicinity will also attract attention.

Returning to the carriage, a drive of 4 or 5m. brings us to a spot which probably most Englishmen have at some time or other desired to visit, and where certainly every pilgrim to Cornwall feels it a sort of religious duty to stand,—the Bolerium of the ancients— the *vanguard* of England against the attacks of the Atlantic—that bold promontory of invincible granite rocks

> " Whose rugged heads look up into the sky,
> Grey as the handle of the scythe of Time "—

THE LAND'S END. Amongst its earliest names have been " The Promontory of Blood," and Pen-von-las (= the end of the earth). Many persons are disappointed at their first sight of the Land's End; but, irrespective of the tempest-scarred cliffs themselves, of columnar granite,

---

* " One Shrubsall (one of Oliver's heroes), then Governor of Pendennis," says Scawen, upset the Mên Amber, near Crowan, a similar natural curiosity, during the days of the Portectorate.

the furious onset of the waves in stormy weather, and
the gorgeous sunsets so frequently to be witnessed from
this point—the associations which cannot fail to present
themselves at such a spot must always invest the Land's
End with a deep and almost melancholy interest. Poets
and painters have lavished the wealth 'of their respective
arts upon the scene; and the visitor who may find any
difficulty in realizing the lessons suggested by the stern
magnificence which surrounds him, will probably find
that difficulty removed if he separates himself for a while
from those by whom he may chance to be accompanied,
and will ponder over the prospect *alone*. With this object
he is recommended to *sleep* at the Land's End—either at
the inn which has recently been built on the summit of
the cliff, or at the "First and Last Inn in England," at
the little village of *Sennen*, about 1m. inland.

c. Should the morning prove clear, a sight may be
obtained of the *Scilly Islands*, 25m. distant, and the
Wolf Rock lighthouse, the latter built 1862-9 at a cost of
over 60,000*l.*, 8m. to the S.E. of Land's End. The
Longships light, which is about 2m. W. of Land's End, is
almost certain to be visible. It was first built of granite
about 1793.* There are many curiously-shaped rocks
along the coast, to which more or less fanciful names
have been given; indeed, should our traveller have time at
his disposal, he will be thoroughly rewarded by a rough
cliff walk from Land's End to the Logan Rock, about
6m., when he will see some of the finest granite cliff
scenery in Cornwall, including Tol-Pedn-Penwith, and
the singular Funnel cavern, of similar origin to the
"Lion's Den" at the Lizard. Assuming, however, that he
adheres to the programme sketched out above, Sennen
Church Town need not detain him long; the Church,
dedicated to St. John Baptist in 1441, Perpendicular, and
restored in 1867, being of no particular interest, except
of its being nearly 400 feet above the sea, and for the story
of the large stone east of the church having formed
a dining table for seven kings some thirteen hundred

* In the autumn of 1877 one of the light-keepers was
washed off the rock and drowned; the same fate having befallen
three at least of his predecessors. Another man died in the
lighthouse; whilst, of two others, one committed suicide, and
another went raving mad. This lighthouse was rebuilt in 1872.

years ago—a tradition which certainly cannot be vouched
for.

The tourist should now prepare for an early start
and a cliff walk northwards to Botallack, of about 8m.
Striking the coast about ½m. W. of *Sennen*, he will come
upon *Maen Castle*, another of those interesting cliff
castles of which Cornwall (especially along its western
shores) possesses so many examples. *Sennen Cove* (½m.
to N.) is soon reached ; and a view is obtained of *Whitesand Bay*, whose sand teems, like that of many other
little bays of this district, with a great variety of rare
and beautiful shells.   Oak trees and remains of deer
have been found beneath the surface.   Here, too, tradition
says, Athelstane, King Stephen, King John, and Perkin
Warbeck have either landed or embarked.   But the traveller is recommended not to linger by the way, although
he would find plenty of raised beaches and other geological
curiosities to detain him.   Passing on his left *Cape Cornwall* (said to be the only "Cape" in England), and
Kenidzhek (= the hooting) *Castle*, he will be delighted to
rest a while, after his 7 or 8 m. walk, at the *Botallack Mine*,
celebrated not only for its submarine works, but also for
its high antiquity, and the wealth and variety of its
mineral treasures.   If he desires to inspect the underground workings of this wonderful example of man's
audacity in searching after wealth, he should provide
himself with credentials, and make all his arrangements
before leaving Penzance.   The descent into the mine is
laborious, and not without danger.   It was, however, to
some extent accomplished by the Prince and Princess
of Wales in 1865 ; and he who accomplishes the feat will
never forget his sensations on hearing the boulders
moved by the waves over his head.   Even those who
do not make the descent, will be astonished at the extra-
ordinary situation of this mine, and the manner in
which its works and engines are constructed, even on
the dizzy edges of the cliffs.   The Levant Mine, about
1m. to the N., is another example of these dangerous
submarine operations.   Another mile further on, in the
same direction, is *Pendeen*, the residence of the famous
but somewhat fanciful Cornish historian and antiquary,
the Rev Dr. Wm. Borlase, F.R.S.   The house bears the
date 1670.

The tourist will, however, probably now be glad, after

his hard day's work, to get back for a night's rest at the somewhat homely accommodation of the Commercial Inn, *St. Just.*

d. In the little market town of ST. JUST, the church, dedicated to St. Justus, should be seen: it is late Perpendicular, and, as in so many other cases in Cornwall, on the site of an older church, whose name was in this case *Lafrouda* (= the church of the cross). An ancient cross, found in an old chapel on Cape Cornwall, and an old stone in the chancel, inscribed "Silus* hic jacet," should be noticed.

The remains of the Plan-an-guare, or the Round, where "miracle plays" used formerly to be represented, are now nearly obliterated; it formerly had six rows of benches. About 1½m. to N.E. are the two stone circles of *Tregeseal* (=? the council house), overlooked by the remarkable pile of rocks called *Karn Kenidzhek* (= the hooting cairn). About 1m. E. are *Chun* or *Chywoon*, castle and cromlech (= the house on the down), the former one of the most perfect of the circular hill-castles of Cornwall. It consists of two concentric walls of Cyclopean masonry, with a space of 30 feet between them. The inner circle contains numerous partitions, and the entrance on the western side was carefully defended. On the north side of the hill may be noticed remains of an ancient British village, known locally as the "Crellas"; and there are also numerous small stone barrows adjacent. The cromlech is an ancient sepulchre, which suggested to the late Charles Chorley the following lines:—

"What mighty dead lies here,
  Lone on this moorland drear,
Where, from o'er Morvah's sullen-moaning seas,
O'er cairn-crowned heights rolls on the unceasing breeze
  In mystic, wild career?

"Haply is here the grave
  Of Briton-warrior brave,
Who, battling boldly for his homeland right,
Vanquished at length by Northmen's slaught'rous might,
  Calm death-sleep here did crave;

---

* St. Justus is said to have been a companion of St. Augustine to England, A.D. 596 (*cf.* Buller's ' St. Just '); and Silus is conjectured to have been one of the companions of St. Petrock into Cornwall in the 5th century.

H

"And deem'd that here might Fame
  To latest years proclaim
His val'rous deeds :—but, faithless to its trust,
Fame hath not left the venerated dust
  The shadow of a name." *

Near at hand is Ding Dong Mine, one of the most
ancient in Cornwall; and 3m. N.E. as the crow flies
is *Mulfra* (= cormorant, or round, bald hill) Quoit or
Cromlech ; and somewhat nearer are another stone circle
of "nine maidens," and the inscribed stone known as the
Maen Scryfa, to the memory of Rialobran, the son of
Cunoval, dating perhaps as early as the 6th century.
The tourist will probably, however, instead of extending
his excursion so far to the east, prefer taking the road
through the wild district of *Lanyon*, which leads him
close to the Lanyon or Giant's Quoit, about 2m. from
Chywoon,—one of the most picturesque and stupendous
monuments of the district of Penwith. The top stone
was thrown down by a storm in 1816, but was replaced
eight years afterwards with the same machinery that
was used to reinstate the Logan Rock. 2½m. farther
on is *Madron*, a small village, 1½m. N.W. of Penzance. The church, dedicated to St. Mary, was formerly the mother church of Penzance ; and here are
kept the early registers of that town. The oldest re-
maining parts of the present church are the lower part
of the tower, and the chancel, 13th century. The font is
Norman. ¼m. N. of the church is the curious baptistery known by the name of *Madron Well* (now, August
1877, in a sadly neglected state), to whose water
miraculous virtues are supposed to attach.

The traveller will now have seen typical examples of
most of the objects in the Land's End district, except
perhaps, of an ancient British village ; of which Bos-
phrennis and Chysauster afford good specimens. These

---

* Mr. Chorley, though not born in Cornwall, spent most of
his life at Truro; where, for many years, he was on the staff
of the 'Royal Cornwall Gazette,' and afterwards edited the
'R. I. C. Journal.' He was a man of the most varied attain-
ments, but was specially devoted to philological studies;
and his loss was severely felt, not only by the small but appre-
ciative circle of friends whom his singularly modest and retiring
disposition privileged with his intimacy, but also by the County
generally.

places lie a few miles to the north of Penzance, and, if time permit, the tourist may take one or both of them in an excursion to *Gulval* Church; the hill of *Castle-an-Dinas* (735 feet high); and *Zennor Cromlech*, probably the largest example in Europe. The tin-smelting works at *Chyandour* are also worth a visit. The works of J. S. Courtney, R. Edmonds, and J. T. Blight contain much valuable information about this most interesting part of Cornwall, and include accounts of its remarkable geology, fauna, and flora.

SCILLY ISLES.

DURING the summer short sea-trips are occasionally
made from Penzance to the Lizard district, thus enabling
visitors to inspect from the sea the interesting coast
line between these two points; but by far the most
attractive marine excursion from Penzance is that to the
Scilly Isles, which may be made almost daily in about
four hours (fares 7s. or 5s.); distance from Penzance
about 36m., or 25m. from the Land's End.* The
steamer starts from Penzance pier, and skirts the coast
so closely, as far as the Land's End, as to enable the
traveller to recognize, under entirely different aspects,
many places with which he is presumed to have already
made himself acquainted. We shall therefore assume
that the Runnel Stone Beacon, the Wolf Rock Fog Bell
and Light, the Longships Lighthouse, and the Seven
Stones Lightship (stationed here in 1841), have been
safely passed—that he has steamed through Crow Sound,
and has landed on the pier of *Hugh Town*, the "capital"
of *St. Mary's, Scilly*. To secure accommodation at the
Hugh House Hotel should be his first endeavour; should
he fail in this, he may "put up" at "Tregarthen's," or
may get a choice of tolerable lodgings.

Probably the etymology of few words has excited
more learned discussion than that of "Scilly;" but the
most probable meaning is one which the position of
these granite islets itself denotes, viz. "cut off." The
circuit of the islands, which are about thirty in number,
is nearly 30m. Only five, *St. Mary's, Trescaw, St. Martin's, St. Agnes*, and *Bryher*, are now inhabited; and it
is proposed to describe the first four of these in the
order named: premising that *St. Mary's* may be seen on
foot, but that a boat is indispensable for the others. A
small pilot-boat is best, as such are manned by at least

* It has recently been decided to lay a postal telegraphic
cable between Scilly and Porth Curnow, near the Land's End.

two hardy and skilful hands*—for even the internal
navigation of Scilly is not without some risk, even under
favourable circumstances. It may be observed that, on
these islands, on an average of the last ten years, thirty-
one lives and 10,000*l.* worth of property are annually
lost: additional beacons, signals, &c., are about to be
erected.

ST. MARY'S. The *Hugh* should first be perambulated:
it is an agreeable promenade—"the Mall of Scilly," as
old Troutbeck called it, and leads completely round the
peninsula—forming a favourite resort of the "Scil-
lonians" (as they prefer being called), and also a fortified
enclosure, along whose *enceinte* various small batteries
will be noticed. On the higher ground stands the
Keep, Star Fort, *alias* Elizabeth Castle, visited by
Queen Victoria in September 1846. The inscription,
E · R · 1593, is over the principal entrance; and a good
general view of the surrounding group of isles may be
obtained from the roof. The tourist should next wend his
way eastwards through the principal street (often flooded
in stormy weather at high water spring tides) of Hugh
Town, where some shipbuilding is carried on, to Peninnis
(= the island head). Here he will find what is probably
the grandest and most fantastic assemblage of granite
rocks in England. It requires little stretch of the imagi-
nation to see amongst the huge masses—contorted by the
violent convulsion which first thrust them through the
earth's crust, and since weather-worn by the storms of
centuries—weird likenesses of primeval monsters of giant
bulk, and "counterfeit presentments" of the elephants,
rhinoceroses, and apes of our own days. Many of the
rocks have recognized names; but the resemblances vary
with different points of view, and the visitor will be
astonished with the variety of suggestive forms which he
will find by wandering for a short time over and around
Peninnis. He should next visit Old Town, the ancient
capital, with some slight remains of a castle, and the old
church, with some curious monuments. The latter is
now only used as a cemetery chapel. Note the numbers

---

* A man called Tom Jenkin, of Hugh Town, will be found,
if not engaged in piloting, a trustworthy and intelligent boat-
man. Provisions should be taken in the boat if a day's cruise
about the islands is contemplated.

of shipwrecked mariners who rest in the churchyard:
the last great addition was made after the wreck of the
'Schiller' in May 1875, on the Retarrier Ledges, when
311 out of 354 persons on board were drowned, and the
value of a quarter of a million sterling went to the
bottom.* *Porthellick* (= the herring cove, cove of willows,
or marshy cove) lies a little farther on in the same
direction; and here is shown the spot where Sir
Cloudesley Shovel's body was thrown ashore: on it, the
natives say, no grass will grow. On the occasion of the
terrible shipwreck, which happened on a foggy evening,
22nd October, 1707, four ships of the squadron returning
from Toulon were wrecked on the western rocks, and
upwards of 2000 persons perished.† Near at hand, on
the rising ground, is a little hollow called Holy Vale,
where there was probably in former times some small
religious establishment: here a few elms, sycamores, and
apple trees grow—rare objects on St. Mary's. Yet the
tourist will be surprised during his walk to see the
enormous size of the geraniums and fuchsias which grow
in front of most of the cottage doors, and the luxuriant
mesembryanthemum which trails over some of the
hedges. This " walk into the country," as it is locally
termed, may be prolonged all round the coast line of
St. Mary's—along the latter part of it may be noticed
remains of some old batteries temp. Henry VIII. and
later—or to the telegraph station, 205 feet above the
sea, from which perhaps the best general view of the
islands may be obtained; or, if he prefer it, the visitor
may inspect the remains of the ancient stone crosses on
Sallakey Hill.

THE ISLE OF TRESCAW (= the place of elder trees) lies
about 2m. N. of St. Mary's Harbour; and a short
walk from the landing place leads to the famed gardens
of the " Lord Proprietor "—now Colonel Dorrien Smith,
the lessee of the Duchy of Cornwall. Mr. Augustus
Smith, his predecessor, will long be remembered in
Scilly as a " benevolent despot" who enforced several
most beneficial reforms amongst the islanders. In

---

* Much of the cargo was afterwards recovered by divers.
† See an interesting account of the event, and of Sir Cloudesley
Shovel, in an official letter by Addison, R. I. C. Journal, vol. i.
p. 64, 1864–5. And *cf.* Lord Stanhope's ' Life of Queen Anne.'

these remarkable gardens will be seen an almost tropical luxuriance : avenues of yuccas and aloes, hedges of geraniums, myrtle, and verbenum *trees*, and innumerable bamboos and dracænas start up on every side, until one almost fails to realize that he is within a short sail from England. In the midst of the gardens are the ruins of the Abbey of St. Nicholas, patron of mariners—an Early English building, formerly a cell of the Abbey of Tavistock. Passing through the gardens along the shore of a small fresh-water lake, 'Dolphin (Godolphin) town is soon reached. This has no attractions; but here it will be necessary to procure a guide should the tourist be desirous of penetrating far into the recesses of *Piper's Hole*, a singular cavern, 600 feet long, on the north side of Trescaw, about which all sorts of strange stories are told as to its subterranean, or rather submarine, communication with another "Piper's Hole" at Peninnis, St. Mary's. Its most noticeable features are its great length, the small lake in its dark interior (on which a padlocked boat is kept), and the roof, which is formed of huge granite boulders.

New Grimsby Harbour—on whose shores are the remains of *Oliver's Castle*, whilst on the top of the hill above it are the ruins of another fort, *Charles Castle*—will recall the times when Scilly was so gallantly held for the King, but was at last surrendered to Blake and Ayscough. At New Grimsby the boat should be waiting; and, without further landing at *Bryher* or *Samson* — unless the fine series of kist - vaens on the summit of the latter island should tempt the tourist—he should now proceed to—

St. Martin's, with its Higher, Middle, and Lower Town. The first named is the principal place, and near it is St. Martin's Church, rebuilt in 1821. The day-mark, which is the only object of interest on this island, is on a fine eminence on the east side, and was erected in 1683 ; but, sooth to say, St Martin's is hardly worth a visit.

St. Agnes—or as it is called in the old records, *Hagenes*, or *Hagness* (thus indicating, perhaps, traces of occupation of these islands by the Northmen)—really consists, at high tides, of two islands. The smaller or eastern one, called Gugh (with many barrows on it), is separated from the larger only by a sandy ridge. The *Lighthouse* should first be seen—it forms a day-mark as well. When first built in 1680, it was illuminated by a huge coal-fire; the old iron cresset is preserved in Trescaw Gardens. The present admirable arrangement of a "revolving" light was introduced in 1790, and is a most ingenious contrivance for throwing upon every point of the horizon the full blaze of its light once a minute. The *Church*—of no architectural interest—was built about forty years ago, on the site of a smaller building: the erection of the original structure does great credit to the inhabitants; the cost having been defrayed by them, according to Drew, from a sum of money received as the salvage of a French vessel wrecked here in 1685;—even the church bell is the result of a shipwreck. In fact, this part of the Scilly Isles has perhaps the most tragic history of all, as may be learnt from the records at the lighthouse. Looking westward to the *Bishop Rock* Lighthouse, 7m. from Hugh Town, there is scarcely an acre of water which has not its melancholy tale to tell. The Bishop Rock Light is described by the Lighthouse Commissioners as "magnificent, and perhaps the most exposed in the world"; the spray in rough weather goes 110 feet over the top. The present building is of granite; it cost over 36,000*l*., and was lit for the first time in 1858; an attempt made in 1849 to build one of iron on this spot was a failure; the whole, when nearly complete, having been swept away by a storm in the following year.

Other islands may be visited if the tourist has plenty of time at his disposal, but the foregoing are the chief points of interest; and it now only remains to give a few general remarks on the Scilly Islands. That they were originally occupied by a Celtic population seems probable from the old names of most of the islets and rocks; and they further appear to have been used by the Romans as a kind of penal settlement. Nowadays, however, the threat towards a recalcitrant islander is (or at any rate till lately *was*) that he shall be "*banished*" to the mainland." The Vikings (with whom Scilly seems to have been a favourite resort) settled here for a short time at the end of the 10th century; and by the middle of the 11th monks took up their abode at *Trescaw*. In the middle of the 14th century Scilly seems to have been a place of refuge for runaway serfs and others. Coming down to the times of Henry VIII., we find Scilly much harassed by the marauding incursions of the French and

Spaniards; and it was not until the succeeding reign, when Elizabeth leased the islands to the Godolphins, that better times for Scilly arrived. The Godolphin-Osborne families continued the Lords under the Crown for more than two centuries and a half, except during the interval of the Commonwealth. Scilly fell into the hands of King William IV. in 1831, shortly after which time St. Mary's Church was built; and, soon afterwards, Mr. Augustus Smith, to whose vigorous administration reference has already been made, became the Viceroy or rather Viceduke—as they are held under the Duchy of Cornwall. The natural history and geology of the islands will be found admirably given in the works of Mr. L. H. Courtney and the Rev. I. W. North, formerly chaplain.

We shall now assume the tourist to have returned to *Penzance*, and to be ready to commence his homeward journey along the *northern* side of the county.

The first point of interest is *St. Ives*, to which there are three modes of approach—viz. *a.* the old road through *Gulval*, leaving Castle-an-Dinas on the left, and thence through Halse Town; *b.* the new road made some years ago through Crowlas, Cannons Town, and Lelant; and *c.* the rail; changing at *St. Erth*, and, if desired, walking thence (about 5m.) to St. Ives; or, if preferred, going on by rail all the way. (The branch to St. Ives was opened 1877.) Perhaps *c.* is on the whole the best method; but the church at *Lelant*, with some Norman portions (rare in Cornwall), is the only object which makes it worth while to walk from St. Erth. *Lelant* (= ? *Les Landes*, or the church by the river) was in former times the trading port of this creek; and some of its houses still wear an old-fashioned look of respectability. On a hill overlooking St. Ives the tourist will notice a granite pyramid, erected in 1782 by a Mr. John Knill, sometime Collector of Customs of St. Ives, as his mausoleum. He left 10*l.* a year for the repair of this monument, for "certain charitable purposes," and for games and dances to be celebrated at the spot on St. James' Day.

[*St. Ives* (anciently Pendinas and Porth Ia.), so named, either from Ia, a female Irish saint of the 5th century, or perhaps from a still earlier bishop, Ivo or Ive, is an old, straggling, and not very inviting town (but improving),

beautifully situated, and at one time a favourite resort of
the fashionables of Penwith. It is chiefly celebrated as
one of the chief places for the pilchard fishery ; indeed
the Returns from 1833 to 1843 show that half the pilchards
exported from Cornwall were from St. Ives. The church,
Early Perpendicular, is good, and has a handsome roof and
good font, and the tower is one of the best in the county.
The churchyard walls are washed by the sea, which is
here encroaching, and about 130 years ago did much
damage to the east windows. Notice a curious cross,
representing on one side the Holy Family, and on the
other the Crucifixion. There are also the remains of a
desecrated chapel of St. Leonard on the old quay. The
Corporation have some interesting insignia, especially
Sir Francis Basset's loving-cup, with its inscribed exhor-
tation to peace and goodwill. *St. Ives* was incorporated
16 Charles I., and first made a parliamentary borough in
1558, but lost one member in 1832. It enjoys the curious
distinction (in Cornwall) of having taken the side of the
Parliament during the Great Rebellion. In 1647 a plague
visited the town, and destroyed one person out of every
three ; the unfortunate inhabitants were supplied with
food brought from the neighbouring parishes to the
margins of two streams of water in which the money for
payment was put, one at Pulmanter, the other at Carbis
Valley. The latter is now a favourite place for picnics ;
and endeavours are being made to render St. Ives itself an
attractive watering-place. It is defended by a 3-gun
battery.]

Returning to the main line at *St. Erth*, the tourist will
soon notice the extensive weirs, quays, reservoirs, and
tide-gates erected by the late Mr. Henry Harvey ; and the
great foundry of HAYLE (= creek)—which has produced
some of the largest steam-engines in the world—the latter
place also the offspring of his energy and genius.* The
blown sands of the "Towans" (= sandhills) on both

---

* The eminent engineer, Richard Trevithick, born in the
neighbouring parish of Illogan, married Mr. Henry Harvey's
daughter, and his duties frequently took him to Hayle. To
Trevithick, whose interesting biography has lately appeared, we
owe the invention "of the high-pressure steam-engine, of the
steam-carriage, and of that boiler without which (or a modifica-
tion of which) no steamboat could have crossed the Atlantic."

sides of the harbour will also claim attention. From these
towans have been excavated Roman coins, the dates
of which seem to prove that the first great accumulation
of sands in this neighbourhood took place before the final
departure of the Romans in the 5th century.

Copperhouse is soon passed on the left—its name indicates its origin; but it was found, after some experience,
that it was cheaper to carry the copper ore to the coal in
South Wales than to bring coal to *Copperhouse.*

[*Gwinear Road* is the station from which the modern
seat of *Pendarves* * (= head of the oak trees), containing
a few Opies, and the more ancient mansion of Clowance
(= the valley of echoes), a residence of the St. Aubyns
since the days of Richard II., may be best visited. They
are both to the right, and about 3m. from Gwinear Road ;
the latter contains, in addition to paintings by foreign
masters, some family portraits by Sir Joshua.]

The tourist, having resumed the rail, in a few minutes
reaches CAMBORNE (= the crooked river), one of the great
mining centres to which reference has been made in the
section on Mines. The church is Perpendicular, and of
no especial interest. From this point, *Tehidy* (3m. N.),
the seat of the Bassets, with its fine park, and pictures
by Gainsborough, Sir Joshua, Lely, Kneller, Vandyke, and
others, may be visited. But probably *Dolcoath* (= the
old pit) *Mine,*† one of the deepest and most ancient in
Cornwall, will prove even more attractive, as this may be
pronounced the best *typical* mine in Cornwall for any visitor
to see whose time is limited. The well-known courtesy
of Captain Pearce will (if circumstances permit) facilitate
the comprehension and the enjoyment of the strange
sights and sounds amongst which the tourist will now
find himself.

Three miles more by rail, and, crossing the " Red
River " (on whose banks about 1½m. below Tucking-

* The late Mr. Pendarves, M.P., was a beneficent friend of
the Cornish miner.

† An excellent model of this mine may be seen at the Museum
of Practical Geology in Jermyn Street, London. It is now more
than 340 fathoms (2040 feet) deep; has sold ore to the value
of 6¼ millions sterling; has paid the lord in dues 312,500*l*., and
never looked better than it does now ; the average value of a
fathom of ground is 150*l*. But there was an outlay of 37,500*l*.
before the mine began to pay.

mill 40,000*l.* worth of machinery has been erected for the purpose of catching the tin which the stream holds in suspension), and *Redruth* is gained; or, if the traveller prefer walking, he may visit, *en route* to that place, the famous hill of *Carn Brea*, from whose summit he may command a view of both channels, and also obtain a general idea of the position and appearance of many of the 'principal mines in this part of Cornwall, such as Dolcoath, Cook's Kitchen, Tincroft, to the west; the numerous "bals" or mines of the Pool and Illogan districts northwards, with St. Agnes Beacon and the Polberrow Consols and Huel * Kitty in the blue distance; to the south are seen the Bassets, Huel Beauchamp, and Huel Buller; and 4 or 5m. to the E. and N.E. the once celebrated Gwennap mining district—now perhaps the most poverty-stricken of all. The Gwennap district comprises Tresavean, where the humane " Man Engine " was first introduced, the Consols, and United Mines, Huel Jewel, Poldice, Creegbraws, Huel Unity, and Huel Busy; with hundreds of others. The scene from Carn Brea was, twenty years ago, one of the busiest in the world: how changed it all is now, none but those who knew it then can tell! Apparently a barren, unprofitable waste; but, even now, richer under the surface than perhaps any other portion of the globe.

Carn Brea (=? the mountain rock) is about 700 feet above the sea; the tourist will be struck with the picturesque granite blocks on its summit. Dr. Borlase and Sir Gardner Wilkinson have described them in great detail; and with an earnestness and vivacity which have often led them and other writers to assert as proven facts what they have merely imagined. Here, it has been said, was the chief scene of Druid worship—here was the sacrificing rock, in the hollows of which (curiously resembling the human figure) the victim was laid—and here were the granite basins hollowed out to receive his blood!

The Castle (mentioned by William of Worcester) was occupied by a Bassett, temp. Edward IV.; its date is involved in obscurity, and clues to its origin have been much confused by modern alterations; there are numerous small square holes in its walls, much like those at Tin-

* Huel = a mine or working; it is now more usually spelt "wheal."

tagel, the precise use of which has not been ascertained. About 200 yards to the S.E. are remains of a circular British earthwork, close to which is a tall monument erected to the memory of Lord De Dunstanville, of Tehidy, in 1836. On the road to Redruth the Church is passed; it was rebuilt about 120 years ago, and is uninteresting.

REDRUTH (= ? tre trot, the place in the river bed) is a town of some antiquity, but derives its importance entirely from the mines by which it is surrounded, and which it supplies from its markets. Most of the weekly "ticketings" or copper ore sales are held here.

[From Redruth (where Tabb's Hotel is the best) the tourist may visit *Portreath* (= sandy cove), a small but busy port, about 4m. to the N.W.; and *Gwennap Pit*, 1½m. E. of Redruth, where Wesley preached during his last visit to Cornwall, in 1781, to many thousand persons.]

Resuming the rail at Redruth Station, in about 2m. we reach *Scorrier Gate*, a good point of departure for *St. Agnes* and *Perranzabuloe*. The road passes through a melancholy district of deserted mines, amongst which may be mentioned Huels Hawk, Rose, and Concord, whose rubbish heaps cover the surface of the ground; next, through the hamlet of *Blackwater*, and then, bearing to the left over *Mingoose Downs*, in about 6m. is reached the primitive village of

St. Agnes, formerly *Breannick* (= ? the place of clay, or the hill by the water), where there is a little church, rebuilt about thirty years ago, with an old font. *St. Agnes* is chiefly interesting from the Beacon, or "Ball," about 1m. to the W., and 621 feet high, from the summit of which fine views are to be obtained. But the most remarkable feature of this hill is its geological formation: 300 or 400 feet above the sea are found clays and sands which nearly encircle the hill, *resting on the slate*, and which have given rise to much learned geological speculation. De la Beche says that these deposits are unique in Cornwall. Of the clay, tobacco pipes were formerly made; and it is also in request for fastening the miners' candles to their hats. 1m. N. of St. Agnes is the *Porth*, at the mouth of Trevaunance Valley, a small port

which has been established at vast expense and after
many failures, on this dangerous part of the coast. It
was attempted in 1632, in 1684, in 1699, in 1710, and was
finally completed in 1794 by a Company of whom the
writer's grandfather was one. There are some curious
caverns near it. In the neighbourhood of *St. Agnes* are
some important tin mines, such as Polberow and Huel
Kitty, of whose produce the old Cornish saying runs :—

> Stean   San Agnes an   guella   stean in   Kernow.
> (The tin of St. Agnes is the best tin in Cornwall.)

The tourist is now recommended to walk 2 m. past *Harmony Cot* (the birthplace of John Opie, a mine carpenter's
son, who rose to be Professor of Painting to the Royal
Academy); and through Perran Coombe (= valley),
another 2m., to

PERRAN PORTH or PERRAN-ZABULOE (= Perran in the
sand), where the "Tywarnhaile Arms" will afford him
homely accommodation. Here the fine beach, 3m. long at
low water, and the numerous caverns and rocks on its
western side are well worth a visit. But on no account
should a visit to the ruins of the ancient *church or oratory*
of the Irish saint Piran, amongst the hills of blown
sand about 2½m. N. of the inn, be omitted. (It may be
desirable for a stranger to take a guide.) This, and a
somewhat similar structure discovered in the sand at
Gwithian, near Hayle, are probably the very earliest
remains of ecclesiastical antiquity in Cornwall. It is
supposed to have been built by St. Piran, who was sent
by St. Patrick to Cornwall as a missionary to the Druidical
pagans in the 4th or 5th century; and to have been overwhelmed and lost four centuries afterwards. Another
church, built as near as possible to it (but a little to the
S.)* early in the 15th century, nearly shared the same
fate, but it was taken down and rebuilt in its present
position, 4m. S. of the old church, in 1803. After having
been lost for about ten centuries, the first church was
discovered in 1835; it is small, being only about 25 feet
by 12½ feet, and of the rudest possible construction: it
is without a font, the baptistery being adjacent. Though
too curious and profane hands have removed some of the
carved stones, the best are preserved in the Truro Museum.

* The site is marked by a cross.

The tourist may now return to *Truro*, either by 'bus or on foot. If he have time, strength, and inclination for the latter (an unfrequented walk of about 10 m.), he will be able to visit, *en route*, *Perran Round*, a circular enclosure, 130 feet in diameter, with seven rows of seats, and capable of holding 2000 persons, where miracle plays used to be performed ; and the interesting hill fortresses of *Karkie Castle* and *Caer Dane*. His approach to Truro would then be through Shortlane's End, and past *Kenwyn* Church, near which is the residence of the Bishop of Truro.

Truro and the railway route between it and *Par* have already been described. We shall therefore assume the tourist to have again arrived at the latter Station, and to be about to proceed by one of the few trains of the Cornwall Minerals Railway to *Newquay*, 20m. to the N.W.

Passing by steep gradients up a picturesque valley, over whose granite rocks a pretty stream tumbles, and noticing some china-clay works by the way, the tourist passes on the right *Luxulyan* (famed for its granite,* specimens of which are exhibited in huge fantastic blocks in the midst of the fields), and in 8m. reaches *Victoria*, the station for

Roche. The church is modern and uninteresting; but the ruins of the little hermit's cell and chapel (Decorated), about 10 feet square, of St. Michael, on the fine pile of granite, about 100 feet high and 680 feet above sea level, known as *Roche Rocks*, are worth a visit. Here Tregeagle finds refuge, after his midnight flight from the devil across the moors from Dozmare Pool. Six miles farther on is *Halloon* (= ? high down), at the opposite extremity of the *Tregoss*, or (locally) *Goss Moor* (= ? the wooded moor), famous for its breed of rough but serviceable ponies, and for the tradition of its having been a favourite hunting-ground of King Arthur. At *Halloon* a 'bus or cart from *St. Columb* (about 3m. N.) meets the train. Another 6m. (or 20m. from *Par*), and the traveller reaches

NEWQUAY (once called Towan Blistra). Newquay,

---

* The Duke of Wellington's tomb, in St. Paul's Cathedral, was made out of a block of granite from Luxulyan, weighing 70 tons.

whose name betrays its modern origin,* is a rising
watering-place, besides being a busy little tidal port, and
an important fishing station. It is charmingly situated,
and has magnificent caverns, beautiful hard sands, and
capital bathing. There are two fair inns—Prout's
and the Red Lion—besides numerous lodging-houses.
A pleasant promenade leads over the Beacon Hill and
past the "Huer's" look-out house to the *Towan Head*,
which stretches boldly out into the Bristol Channel, and
commands good views up and down the coast; this headland has, moreover, some interesting raised beaches and
trap dykes for the geologist. *Fistral Bay* extends
about 1m. S. of the Head, and has a fine, but exposed,
sandy beach. Where the isthmus connects the Head
with the mainland may be seen (near the fish-cellars),
the commencement of an attempt by the late Mr. Treffry
to form a breakwater and a cut, with a view to making a
large, sheltered harbour, available at all times of the
tide—an accommodation of which the north coast of
Cornwall is sorely in need. This undertaking was unfortunately put an end to—at any rate for the present—
by Mr. Treffry's death. The "Tea Caverns," formerly
used as smugglers' caves, are in the cliffs under the
look-out house; they are worthy of a visit, and not
difficult of access; but lights should be taken. Pleasant
trips may be made from Newquay to *Crantock* (2½m.
S.W.) across the *Gannel*; and (about the same distance) along the sands to *Trevalga Head*, a detached
cliff to the N.E. extremity of the bay. This should be
so timed, if possible, as to reach Trevalga Head about
eleven o'clock on the day after full or new moon, when
the tides are lowest, and the visitor is thus enabled
to see the magnificent caverns here. Amongst many
other floral rarities of the neighbourhood the white
betony (*Stachys betonica*) has been noticed by a recent
visitor.

The tourist is now recommended to make one of the
most pleasant and varied excursions yet taken in Cornwall; namely, to *Bedruthan Steps*, *Mawgan*, and St. Columb
Major. In order to do this to the greatest advantage, he

---

* The present quay was built about forty years ago; but
Thomas Stuer applied for leave to erect a pier here, and another
at St. Columb Porth, as early as 1615.

should drive, as the route is a long one of nearly 14m.; and he should be at *Bedruthan Steps* (7m.) at eleven A.M., for the same reason as above given with respect to Trevalga Head. Passing (2m.) the sandy Porth of St. Columb Minor, through which runs a little trout stream, and ascending the hill, he will (½m.) notice on his left, close to the edge of the cliff, two large tumuli which were opened three or four years ago, and which exhibit an admirable example of kist-vaens, or stone graves. The westernmost contained fragments of an unburnt human skull; the other a contracted human skeleton and stone hatchet. Another 2½m. and *Mawgan Porth* is reached: here two other small trout streams unite, and join the sea. Ascending another hill, the traveller will notice traces of an old canal, constructed between eighty or ninety years ago for the purpose of conveying sand, as a manure, to the inland farms; but the scheme was a failure. Then, passing through Trenance, in about 2m. is reached perhaps the finest cliff scenery in Cornwall, viz.

Bedruthan Steps, probably so called from the steps which have been cut in the face of the cliff down to the beach, rather than (as some have supposed) from the ladders which have been fixed for mining operations on the precipices at the south extremity of the beach. The finest caverns are at this end, and no time should be lost in visiting them; the approach is somewhat difficult, over a mass of fallen rocks which, till 1866, formed a stupendous natural bridge overhead. A watchful eye must be kept on the waves, lest the tourist's retreat be cut off by the rising tide. The northern portion of this fine beach is studded with beautiful rocks, some of curious forms; one of them bearing a marked resemblance to good Queen Bess. On reascending the cliff he should notice the remains of a cliff-castle, with its triple entrenchment, above Red Cove; and here the tired traveller will doubtless be glad to rest awhile, enjoying at once the unrivalled prospect before him, and the refreshments with which (it is to be hoped) he has furnished himself before leaving Newquay — for there is absolutely *no* " accommodation for man and beast" at *Bedruthan.**

A pleasant drive of about 3½m. back through

* There is also a fine cliff walk of about 12m. from Bedruthan to Padstow, *viâ* Trevose Head.

I

Mawgan Porth now conducts us to the far-famed *Vale of Lanherne* * (? = the iron-stone church), in which, by the banks of a little trout stream, lie *Mawgan* Church and a *Nunnery* embowered amongst trees, which seem doubly beautiful in a district where they are so rare.

MAWGAN (=? mor gan, by the sea). The church (Perpendicular), recently restored, is interesting ; the Arundel brasses, the screen, and carvings are particularly worth notice. In the churchyard will be seen a remarkably beautiful sculptured cross comprising numerous figures ; and, close by, the stern of a boat, wrecked thirty years ago in Beacon Cove (2m. W. of the church), which has been utilized as the monument of ten unhappy men who drifted ashore in her one winter morning, frozen to death. *Lanherne Nunnery* is an old mansion of the Arundels, on the slope of the hill just above the church to its S.

> "Gloomy Lanherne! Thy misanthropic walls
> Strangely with this glad scenery contrast,"

sings Mr. Stokes; yet we are free to confess that there is a certain melancholy softness and privacy about this spot *not* out of harmony with the lives of the eighteen or nineteen nuns who have elected to spend their days immured in sad and strict seclusion. The "lone manse" was devoted to its present purpose about seventy or eighty years ago, by one of the Arundel family, and strangers are admitted to see the plain little chapel only : this is now being restored. There is a small burial ground in front of the chapel door, and an old stone cross, removed hither from Gwinear; but notwithstanding the interest attaching to the spot, Mawgan, from its low situation and sad associations, has a somewhat depressing effect upon the spirits. Departing, therefore, and climbing a stiff hill, we pass on the left (1½m.) *Carnanton*, once the seat of Charles I.'s Attorney-General, Noy ; and (in another 2½m.) gain

ST. COLUMB (so called from a sainted Irish virgin of the 5th century), an old-fashioned little Cornish town, with a market dating from the days of Edward III., and a comfortable, old-fashioned Cornish inn, the Red Lion. Here the tourist should not forget to see the huge silver

* Charmingly described in an illustrated poem of that name by Mr. H. S. Stokes, now of Bodmin, Clerk of the Peace to the county of Cornwall.

punch-bowl presented to Polkinghorne (father of the
present landlord) in recognition of his three hours'
gallant wrestling match with Cann, the Devon champion,
at Tamar Green, near Devonport, on 27th October, 1826.
The fairness of the falls which Polkinghorne administered
to his clever opponent was a matter of dispute amongst
those present, and Polkinghorne was withdrawn by his
committee.* The *church* (partly Decorated and partly
Perpendicular), which is large and handsome, was restored
about ten years ago, and contains some Arundel brasses :
the materials of the lofty tower are said to have directed
Cookworthy's attention to the discovery of the means of
making porcelain. The rectory is a square, moated
dwelling, once a college for ecclesiastics. About 2m.
S.E. of St. Columb is *Castle-an-Dinas*, on a hill 730 feet
high ; a large circular earthwork, with four concentric
ramparts. According to tradition, this was a favourite
hunting-seat of King Arthur.

From St. Columb a coach runs every morning at eight
to *Launceston*, doing the journey in about five hours.
The tourist who wishes to proceed to Launceston direct
would do well to avail himself of it ; or even if he desires
to make *Wadebridge* a halting-place, as the road across
St. Breock Downs between St. Columb and Wadebridge
(8m.), though it commands some extensive views (best
seen from the top of a coach), has no object of interest
save perhaps (at nearly half the distance) a curiously
arranged group of stones called the Nine Maidens,
situated about ¼m. to right of the road.

WADEBRIDGE (=the ford bridge) is celebrated for its
long and ancient bridge of seventeen arches, said to be
the largest in the county. It is a furlong in length, and,
according to Sir J. MacLean, was built some time during
the reign of Edward IV. by a vicar of the neighbouring
church of *Eyloshayle*, named Lovybond, whose sympathies
were aroused by the great loss of life at the ford. The
river Camel is navigable only at spring tides.

From Wadebridge the tourist may, if necessary (on
market days only, Wednesday and Friday), proceed to

---

* The present Cornish champion is Samuel Rundle, who
offers to wrestle, for not less than 50l. a side, with any man in
the world, and allow him one stone weight. (The courtly Carew
describes the champion wrestler of his time as his " friend, John
Goit.")

Bodmin by a small goods line; or he may regain the main line at that town by means of a 'bus, which runs daily from *Padstow*, through Wadebridge, to Bodmin. A 'bus also goes to Padstow in the evening (about 8m.) through Wadebridge.

About 1m. up the valley from Wadebridge is *Egloshayle* (= the church on the creek). The north and east walls are Early English, the rest is Perpendicular; the fine 3-stage tower and south aisle being probably the work of the philanthropic builder of the bridge—whose appropriate rebus, three hearts bound round by a cord, is displayed over the tower door. The church was restored in 1867, and contains perhaps the only example in Cornwall of an old stone pulpit. Three miles farther on is Pencarrow, the beautifully wooded seat of the distinguished old Cornish family of Molesworth. Notice the magnificent hedge-banks for which, here and elsewhere, Cornwall is so deservedly famed.

[From Wadebridge the tourist may proceed, either by river (if the tide suits) or by road, through *St. Issey* and *Little Petherick* (church rebuilt lately) to

PADSTOW, formerly known by various names, as Aldestow, Oldestow, and Patrickstow, Laffennack, Lodenek, Petrockstow—the last being its name down to the time of Henry VIII.—a maritime town which has a strong family likeness (both as to its merits and demerits) to *St. Ives*. Padstow supplied two ships for the siege of Calais, temp. Edward III., and was once a place of more importance than at present (though the port still has about 100 vessels), owing to the silting-up of the mouth of the harbour with sand:* this renders the entrance often difficult and dangerous, as ships have to be most carefully and ingeniously warped in round the Stepper Point; but there is some chance of the harbour being improved. Leland describes it as a "good quick fischar toun, but onclenly kepte," and few will dispute his accuracy. The *haven* is said to supply nearly one-fourth of the sand used for agricultural purposes in Cornwall; it is defended by a modern 2-gun battery. The *church,* lately restored, is dedicated to St. Petrock, a disciple of St. Patrick; it is late Decorated, and is of no great interest.

* The local tradition is that Padstow Bar is due to the dying curse of a mermaid, who was shot in the bay.

The Norman font, on which figures of the twelve apostles are carved, is, however, curious. There have been other religious foundations here; as at *Place House* or *Castle*, the seat of the Prideaux family—a well-situated Elizabethan mansion, containing, amongst other pictures, some early works of Opie. There is steam communication between Padstow and Bristol weekly, the steamer calling at Ilfracombe. A pleasant excursion may be made from Padstow across the penny ferry to *Rock*, for the lately restored church of *St. Enodoc*, rescued, like that of Perranzabuloe, from the blown sand, of which there are such vast tracts on the north-west coast of Cornwall. Thence there is a pleasant ramble of 1½m. to *Polzeath Beach, Hayle Bay*, where lodgings may be obtained.]

Returning to *Wadebridge*, and, if practicable, resuming the coach, the tourist has now before him a delightful drive of about 12m. to *Camelford*, great part of the road being through a beautifully wooded valley along which the Kestell, a trout stream, rushes, and whose sylvan scenery fully compensates for the dearth of objects of historic and antiquarian interest.

CAMELFORD * (= the ford of the camel or crooked river. The camel, which forms the weathercock on the Town Hall, built 1806, owes its proud position to mistaken etymological views). It is a quaint little Cornish town on the slope of a steep hill, and is of considerable antiquity, having been made a free borough as early as 1259. From the time of Edward VI. to 1832 (when it was disfranchised) Camelford returned two M.P.s; and amongst its representatives have been the author of 'Ossian,' and Lords Lansdowne and Brougham. Camelford (The King's Arms Inn) is a good headquarters for excursions to (a) the *Delabole* Slate Quarries; (b) *Brown Willy* and *Roughtor*, the Cornish mountains; and (c) to some picturesque rocky valleys 3 or 4 m. to the S. The angler will also be able to get fair trout fishing in the *Camel*, which flows through the lower part of the town; and still better—though the trout are small — in the *Inny*, about 4m. to the N., in order to reach which he should walk to *Davidstow*. Another pleasant stroll is to *Lanteglos* Church (partly Norman and partly Decorated and Per-

* Camelford also appears in old writings under the names of Gafulford, Cablan, and Cambala.

pendicular), prettily situated in a valley 1½m. W. of
Camelford, where he will find, preserved in the church
and rectory grounds, some interesting fragments of
ancient crosses—one especially of the 11th century, " for
Ælwyne's soul"—and a "Saxon" font; most of them
rescued from ignoble uses or positions by the care of
the late Rev. J. J. Wilkinson.

2m. N. of Camelford is *Worthyvale*, near *Slaughter-
bridge*, on the banks of the *Camel*—the traditional scene
of the great and final conflict between Arthur and his
rebellious nephew, Modred, when the latter was slain,
and the former mortally wounded. But it seems probable
that the great fight—of which traces have been discovered in turning over the soil—was that which took
place nearly three centuries later between the Britons
and Saxons in 823, described in the ' Saxon Chronicle,'
and by Henry of Huntingdon, and others.

[a. *Delabole* (= ? the clay hole, or barren spot) 2½m.
W. of Camelford, is perhaps the largest, best, and most
ancient slate quarry in existence; and is well worth a
visit. The tourist should endeavour to procure a guide
on the spot, who will explain the machinery, the system
of working, &c. The greatest depth of the quarry is
about 300 feet, so that from the surface men at the
bottom seem mere specks. Improvements in machinery
are gradually reducing the numbers employed, and this
machinery is deserving of special notice. The slate, of
which it is said that nearly 150 tons are raised daily, is
not only sent to various parts of this kingdom, but also to
the Continent, and even to America. A specimen of the
rock crystal, or "Cornish diamond," found occasionally
in hollows of the slate, will form an interesting souvenir
of this remarkable spot. Carew says they were once in
great request for jewellery by the old Cornish families ;
and Drayton describes them as

" By nature neatly cut, as by a skilful hand."

b. *Brown Willy*, a corruption of Bron uhella (= the
highest hill), and *Row Tor* (= the rough tor, or the
King's tor), are the two Cornish "mountains" whose fine
outlines (especially that of the latter) have frequently
ere this been visible in the distance; and should certainly,
if the weather be fine, be visited and ascended. The
former is the highest hill in Cornwall, viz. 1380 feet,

whilst Row Tor is 1296 feet above the sea. This
excursion will occupy a day, if properly carried out.
The nearest point to which a carriage can be driven is
the *Landavery Rocks*, about 4m. E. of Camelford. Thence
a rough walk of 2m., over stony and boggy ground,
leads to the top of the higher hill, up which horses are
sometimes ridden. Arrived at the summit, a view of half
the county is commanded Looking southwards, on the
extreme left is Rame Head, with Dozmare Pool glittering
in the middle distance: to the left the Dodman in the
English Channel, and St. Agnes Beacon in the Bristol
Channel close the prospect; whilst Bodmin and the St.
Stephens china-clay works, and the silver stream which
winds along its sandy bed between Wadebridge and
Padstow, stand out in intermediate positions. Turning
to the north, Lundy Isle may be discerned 45m. off,[*]
Davidstow Church, Bude Bay, and Morwenstow forming
the connecting links in this direction: to the left may be
seen the Delabole Quarries, and, beyond them, Port Isaac
Bay, with the jagged tors of Row Tor in the foreground.
To the east rises the splendid panorama of the granite
ranges of the Dartmoor hills, rugged and grey. In the
stone cairn which crowns this isolated summit, the writer
found a nest of wild bees in the autumn of 1877. *Row
Tor*, on whose summit in 1371 was a chapel (the
foundations of which may still be traced on the
most easterly of the two peaks), is also worth ascending (though the prospect is of course very nearly
the same), on account of the strange form of the rocks.
The names and heights of the two principal adjacent hills
to the south and south-east are *Garrah*, 1060, and *Tober*
(or Two Barrow) Hill, 1122 feet: on the sides of most of
these eminences may be noticed traces of their early
British occupants, in the shape of hut-circles, villages,
and cattle-folds. "Arthur's Hall," a small rectangular
enclosure 1m. S.W. of the top of Garrah, will afford
much food for speculation. Was it the site of a church,
a reservoir for water, a cattle-pen, or a place of assembly
of the Ancient Britons?

c. This excursion is also a very rough one, and can
perhaps be best performed by the angler, whose pursuit

[*] Wallis, in the 'Cornwall Register,' states that one night
the ordnance surveyors saw the lights of Swansea in this direction—a distance of 70 miles.

will ensure the proper costume for a rude scramble
amongst some of the wildest and most picturesque scenes
in Cornwall. He should follow south, for about 8m.,
the valley of the Camel to Wenford Bridge — the terminus of a short tramway, which is a branch of the railway
between Bodmin and Wadebridge—and he should also
ascend for a short distance the valleys of its two principal
tributaries, the Hannon and De Lank rivers, both of
which rise at the foot of the hills just described. He
will have a most fatiguing day, but we think one which
will amply repay him.]

Having exhausted the neighbourhood of Camelford,
the tourist should next arrange to proceed (about 6m.)
to one of the most interesting spots in Cornwall, whether
regarded from its legendary and historic associations, or
whether the traveller's object be the magnificent scenery
afforded by the ancient slate precipices which here con-
front the Atlantic rollers. For here

> "The dark cliffs beetle coldly o'er the deep,
> Fringed by the lace-work of frail threaded foam
> That mermaids weave and hang along the shore."

Perhaps nowhere along the Cornish coast can the
everlasting war which is being waged between sea and
land be better seen than in the district which lies about
6m. N.W. of Camelford, and which has for it head-
quarters

TINTAGEL, formerly Dundagil, or Dondagel (= the im-
pregnable fortress). There is a fair inn here, 'The
Wharncliffe Arms'; and a boarding-house kept by J.
Fry; and there are two or three cottages in the village in
which visitors may be accommodated on an emergency—
for the inhabitants are beginning to discover that their
abode and neighbourhood are full of attractions to the
traveller.

And, indeed, it would be difficult to find a place in
Cornwall where there is so much to be seen, both inland
and along the shore: but our limits will compel us to
be brief. The great object of interest is, of course, the
castle—"King Arthur's Castle"—sometimes, according to
the old stories, visible, at others hidden from mortal
gaze. Here, tradition says, "the blameless king" held
his court, and here the Knights of the Round Table

assembled. It was from Tintagel that Arthur sallied to
meet the traitor Modred; it was to Tintagel that he
retired, wounded to death, to be transported to the
" island Valley of Avilion." * The Cornish peasant still
tells how the spirit of the King yet hovers in the form of
that rare bird, the chough † (rare even in Leland's days),
round scenes which, when viewed on the wild spot itself,
are scarcely more real than Guinevere and Launcelot,
Merlin and " lissome Vivien," and Tristram and Isolt
have become for us under the magic touch of the Poet
Laureate, and the pens of the old chroniclers.

Wending our way ½m. westward from the village the
Castle is soon reached—one half on " the island," the
other on the mainland. The latter part should be
visited first; and the tourist should, in order to avoid
the necessity of returning up the valley, procure the key
of the castle from Baker (the janitor appointed by the
Rev. Prebendary Kinsman, vicar of Tintagel and Constable of the Castle), who lives at the little cottage—once
a water-mill—on the banks of the valley stream. Arrived
at the courtyard of the landward part of the castle, he
may realize the lines of the late Rev. R. S. Hawker of
Morwenstow :—

> " Thou seest dark Cornwall's rifted shore,
>   Old Arthur's stern and rugged keep;
> There, where proud billows dash and roar,
>   His haughty turret guards the deep.

> " And mark yon bird of sable wing,
>   Talons and beak all red with blood,—
> The spirit of the long-lost king
>   Passed in that shape from Camlan's flood ! "

It is necessary to descend into the valley again, and to
pass the " porth " (where the curious arrangements for
dropping boats into the sea with cranes and chains should

---

* The Bretons maintain that Arthur was buried, not at
Glastonbury, but on an islet called Agalon, or Avalon, off the
N.W. shores of Brittany.

† Upton's ' Heraldry ' notes the frequent appearance of the
chough in Cornish coats-of-arms as early as 1440. Cox (1720)
gives Pyrrhocorax a very bad character ;—says he is not only
a thief, but an incendiary, and will " privately set houses on
fire."

be noticed) before the only path which leads to the island portion of the castle can be gained. And here, as well as from both eminences, the tourist may consider the claims of two rival theories as to the original plan of the fortress. Some have held that the great chasm between the two portions was once solid ground; and that the present remains formed part of one continuous structure, but that the sea has washed away the intervening portions (Leland tells us that in his time, Henry VIII., the two parts were connected by a drawbridge). Others contend that the two parts are not only distinct, but of different dates; the island portion, or the greater part thereof, being by far the more ancient. Our own opinion is (whatever that may be worth), that at any rate portions of the island structure, and of the mainland buildings, are *both* older than many other parts of the masonry on both sides of the chasm. Doubtless the cliffs have crumbled away on both sides; but we cannot help thinking that there was *always* a "tête-de-pont" on the mainland (of which the circular look-out tower, on that side, formerly was part), and that there was *always* a gap, which was once much narrower than it is now, between it and the island half, and which could be bridged over, for a friend, or be denied to a foe. If this view be correct, it will help to explain, in some degree at least, the strange position chosen for this strong work of defence. It doubtless was a place of perfect safety, from which the ancient defenders of North Cornwall could sally forth on an enemy who approached along the old roads, from the E. and N.E. (of which numerous traces are still visible); or to which they could confidently retire when pressed, knowing that their base was safe, for it was guarded by the sea, which was accessible for friendly barks bringing supplies. Its *history*, of course, begins with much later times (though its advantages long remained the same), and has been carefully summarised from the old writers by Sir John MacLean, in his 'Trigg Minor.'

Geoffry de Monmouth, in the middle of the 12th century, says, "It is situated upon the sea, and on every side surrounded by it; and there is but one entrance into it, and that through a strait rock, which three men shall be able to defend against the whole power of the kingdom."

William of Worcester, in 1478, thus describes it:

"Castrum Tyntagelle fortissimum dirutum prope Camel-ford ubi Arthurus fuit conceptus."

Leland, writing nearly sixty years later, is more explicit. He says, "From Bossinny to Tintagel Castel on the shore a mile. This castelle hath bene a marvelus strong and notable forteres, and almost *situ loci inex-pugnabile*, especially for the dungeon, that is on a great and terrible cragge environed with the se, but having a drawbridge from the Residew of the castelle onto it. There is yet a chapel standyng withyn this dungeon of S. Ulette *alias* Uliane. Shepe now fede within the dungeon. The Residew of the Buildings of the castel be sore wether beten and in ruine, but it hath beene a large thinge. This castel stondith in the paroche of Trevenny and the paroch thereof is of St. Symphorian, ther caulled Simiferian."

Again:

"Wyth yn iiij myles of the sayd Camylford, apon the North Clif ys Tintagel, the which castel had be lykeod iij Wardes, whereof ij be woren away with gulfyng yn of the se, in so much that yt hath made ther almost an isle, and no way ys to enter ynto hyt now but by long elme trees layde for a bryge. So that now withowte the isle rennith alonly a gate-house, a walle, and a fals braye dyged and walled. In the isle remayne old walls, and in the est part of the same, the grownd beyng lower, remayneth a walle embateled, and men alyve saw ther yn a postern dore of yren. Ther is yn the isle a pretty chapel, with a tumbe on the left syde. Ther ye also yn the isle a welle, and ny by the same is a place hewen out of the stony grownde to the length and brede of a man. Also ther remayneth yn the isle a grownd quadrant-walled as yt were a garden plot. And by this walle appere the ruines of a vaulte."

Towards the end of the 16th century several authors refer to it. First among them is Holinshed: "I shall conclude my account of this castle with the information of a worthy friend of mine, who, in his travels into these parts, went purposely to visit it. The ruins of some works, as he tells me, are here to be seen on the tops of two high rocks that stand to the sea; one of them was formerly surrounded by it, and continues to bear the name of an island, but great part of it, by length of time, having fallen down, hath made a neck of land which hath joined it to the other. It is a rock of stupendous height, containing about thirty acres of pasture, and is so very steep and difficult, that it is hard to be conceived how it is possible the sheep should keep their footing, and not fall into the sea as they ascend and descend."

Camden, writing about the same time, says:

". . . Upon the neighbouring shore stands Tindagium (the birthplace of great Arthur), part of it, as it were, on a little tongue thrust out, and part upon an island formerly joined to the mainland by a bridge. They now call it Tindagel; though nothing is left but the splendid ruins of an ancient stately castle."

Carew, a little later, says:

"Tintagel, more famous for his antiquity than regardable for his present estate, abutteth likewise on the sea, yet the ruins argue it to have been once no unworthy dwelling for the Cornish princes. The cyment, wherewith the stones were layd, resisteth the fretting furie of the weather better than the stones themselves. Halfe the buildings were raised on the continent, and the other halfe on an island, continued together (within men's remembrance) by a drawbridge, but now divorced by the downfalne steepe cliffes on the further side, which, though it shut out the sea from his wonted recourse, hath yet more strengthened the late island."

Norden closely follows Carew, and gives a view of the castle, showing the island as almost separate from the mainland, but he describes, as existing, "ye istmos" in the view.

The word "island" is a figurative expression. It is really, and probably always has been, a peninsula. The site and plan of the castle show it to be hardly Norman, though parts of it may be even later; if British, it would have been in ruins before the Conquest, whence, probably, the reason why Tintagel is not mentioned in Domesday, nor in a grant of the manor early in 13th century. The "loop-holes," or putlog-holes, are similar to those at Carn Brea; and are not easily explained. There was a great landslip in 1820, and another in 1846, which carried away part of the wall on the mainland; the fragments are still to be seen trembling on the slope.

On approaching from the landward, attention is first attracted by the great gate, ditch, and fausse-braie.

There was formerly stabling for eight horses in a shed on the right, whilst steps lead up to the ancient look-out tower on the left. There was a slighter west wall over-hanging the sheer cliff, and attached to this were small buildings, with a terrace walk outside. On the island side, up which there is a steep ascent by a zigzag path, maintained under the careful directions of the present Constable, there are remains of a curved "garreted" wall, enclosing buildings which were once the lodgings of the Constable and the Priest, and protecting them, as well as the rest of the garrison, from any foe who might be hardy enough to effect a landing. The iron gate, "Porth Hern," guarded against such an endeavour on the north-east side of the island ; and it was this part which Sir Richard Grenville was so anxious to strengthen, as appears by his report to the Council, and his plan of 1583. On the high ground of the interior of the island are still to be seen traces of the chapel with its altar, the garden, walled, and the "fayre spring of water," which Sir Richard shows in his plan. The view from the island on a fine day baffles description : it must be seen to be realized ; and here the tourist may well spend a long summer afternoon with 'The Idylls of the King' as his sole companion.

In 1245 the Earl of Cornwall sheltered David, Prince of Wales here; but it is uncertain if John de Northampton, the contumacious Lord Mayor of London, was imprisoned here, as is generally supposed. The Earl of Warwick certainly was in 1397. Tintagel Castle was habitable in 1360 (temp. Edward III.), as the Council then ordered that Tintagel and other castles should be supplied with provisions. In 1364 Edward III. issued a mandate to the Constable to keep up the chantry by surrendering his fees to the chaplain, who was to be "stirred up" to reside therein. Lord Burleigh abolished the office of Constable in the middle of the 16th century ; and in 1708 the premises fell into the hands of the Duke of Cornwall, and were leased to various persons as before, but since 1844 they have been retained in the hands of the Duchy.

Another object of interest is the *Church*, standing on the edge of the cliff. It is dedicated to St. Materiana (or Mertheriana) and is one of the most ancient churches in the county, whether we believe or not that portions of it are of Saxon workmanship. It stands, like many of its sister churches, on the long line of the northern Cornish coast; a landmark for the mariner, and a reminder of Him at whose " word the stormy wind ariseth," and Who also " maketh the storm to cease, so that the waves thereof are still." It was restored about seven years ago, but under such careful superintendence that the most vigorous opponent of " restorations" can find little, if anything, to complain of. It preserves its cruciform plan, and formerly had a *central* tower, since replaced by one of much later date (Late Perpendicular) at the west end; from many points of view, however, especially from points in the Boscastle road, the tower *seems* to fall into its original position. The most noticeable features are the following:—The north and south porches, both Norman, and perhaps subsequent to the nave; but the former, which has a solid tympanum, is probably the earlier of the two; the long south aisle with the original stone benches round great part of it, as at the old Church of St. Perran in the Sands; the "Ladye Chapel" (now the vestry) with its stone altar, in the angle between the north transept and the chancel; the massive and venerable Norman chancel arch, with its rudely carved abaci, partly of the same pattern as on one of the sculptured altar stones in the Castle chapel; and the very remarkable Norman font, figured by Lysons and by Sir John MacLean. The corbels or brackets for images or candles, near certain of the windows and the north door, should also be noted; as well as the Decorated eastern sepulchre or founder's tomb, of great interest, on the south side of the chancel; a sculptured coffin-lid, temp. Edward I.; and a small early 15th-century brass for Johanna Boñ.

The bleak, bare churchyard contains little of interest save the base of an old cross, and the upright tombstones supported against the winter storms. The tall mounds, which some imaginative writers have converted into sepulchral tumuli, are merely heaps of rubbish, the results of alterations to the church. One ponderous white monument, as close to the edge of the cliff as it could be placed within the enclosure, should be noticed: it contains the mortal remains of Mr. J. D. Cook, once the accomplished editor of the 'Saturday Review,' with whom Tintagel was a favourite spot, and who built for himself the stone villa in the village fronting the approach from Tregatta.

The vicar, the Rev. Prebendary Kinsman, resides at the Vicarage house, a building of comparatively modern construction, though the interior is "an example of comfort and refinement, through the taste and artistic feeling of the present vicar." It is situated in the valley between the church and the village of Trevena, and is to a considerable extent shut off from the public road by a lofty medieval wall, through which, by a large gateway under a four-centred arch, you enter a pleasant, well-sheltered garden, or pleasure ground, in which is an ancient columbarium, "a pigeon house, made all of stone," as Sylvester Sweetsir, then vicar, described it in 1679. It will readily be understood that, in such a situation and amongst such surroundings, the vicarage has during the summer season many callers; and it is difficult to understand, considering the numerous local calls upon Mr. Kinsman's attention, his duties as a senior county magistrate, and as a beneficent employer of labour in the cliff slate-quarries, how he contrives to welcome graciously the constant and increasing stream of visitors, of every degree, who invade his privacy during the season.

Writing of the borough of Tintagel, Bossinny, and Trevena, Sir John MacLean observes :—"It is somewhat singular that not a single borough in the county of Cornwall is mentioned in the Domesday Survey, notwithstanding that there were twenty-one boroughs entitled to send burgesses to Parliament, besides several others not so privileged, before some of them were, in this particular, partially or wholly disfranchised." He adds then :—"This borough would appear to have arisen with, and to have fallen into decay in like manner as the castle." Leland, writing circa 1540, says :—"This Bossinny hath been a bygge thing for a fishcher town, and hath great privileges graunted onto it. A man may se the ruines of a great numbre of houses."

At Trevena (the name of the village) the Post-office is the most picturesque of the houses that remain, and it has afforded many an artist a subject for his pencil.

There are many delightful excursions to be made from Tintagel, amongst which may be noted :—

a. A walk S. (3m.) along the cliffs to Trebarwith Strand, noticing by the way the quarryings for slate on the cliffs' edge.

b. Another cliff walk of about 3½m. N.E. to Boscastle.

c. A walk to Bossinney, Bossinney Cove, and Rocky Valley.

d. A walk to St. Nighton's Kieve and Trevalga Church; besides other rambles to such points of interest as Pentaley Cross, an ancient Christian monument at the cross-roads, 1m. E. ; Trenaile Bury, a British earthwork, in a field about ½m. S. of the Cross ; or a longer and rougher road to Cadon, or Godolghan Barrow, 4m. E. of Tintagel, 1000 feet above the sea, and commanding a grand view of the surrounding country.

As to a, we have only to mention that the tourist should, if possible, endeavour to reach Trebarwith at low-water spring tides, when there is a fine beach ; he may return by "the Valley Sand road," and through the little hamlets of Trenow and Tregatta. There is no inn here.

b. The pedestrian should prepare himself for a rough walk along the edge of the cliff, commencing at Tintagel Porth. He should first go to the point of Barras Nose (a likely spot for Cornish choughs, which in the distance "show scarce so gross as beetles"); thence by the lofty Tintagel Willapark (= look-out), the fine twin rocks, the Sisters, and the terrible Lye Rock, on which a few sheep are still fed, being hoisted up by ropes to crop the sweet but scanty herbage that grows there. He will now have to make two short inland detours, to avoid the stiff descents into Bossinney Cove and Rocky Valley ; but regaining the coast near Treworthat Farm, he will pass Long and Short Islands, the Black Pit (a frightful chasm), and rounding Boscastle Willapark, on which are traces of an earthen "cliff castle," will wind, by an easy road, up the strange little harbour of Boscastle, and gladly find rest and refreshment at the comfortable inn, 'The Wellington.' He may either drive back to Tintagel or walk by road (about 3½m.) past Forrabury and Trealga.

c. Is a stroll of—first, 1m., to the ancient borough of Bossinney, another of the disfranchised Cornish towns for which eminent men have sat in Parliament. An ancient British earthwork, of unusual height, now surmounted by the village weathercock, is the most conspicuous object in the village. On this mound the formalities of the elections of former days used to take place, sometimes conducted (so it is whispered) by Mayors who, either from knowing the words of the writ by heart, or from not knowing how to read at all, held it upside-down during the ceremony. Mr. McLauchlan thus describes the fort in the R. I. C. J.:—

"There is a rampart and a ditch of a circular form, having more the appearance of an enormous tumulus than a mere camp. The rampart is about 100 feet in diameter, and on the west side there is an outwork about 100 feet square, with the angles rounded off apparently; but the remains are too obscure to allow of its being traced with certainty.* The rampart of the interior, or circular part, seems to have been much higher than that of the exterior work, and to have commanded it. The whole work resembles the camp at Sedberg on the Rotha, and Hornby on the Lune. On the east side is a copious spring, which is dammed back and forms a pond at the head of the brook which falls into the sea at Bossinney Haven." There is a very picturesque ruined cottage at its rear.

At the north end of the village a little field-road leads down to Bossinney Cove, where, it is said, a monk once vainly attempted to establish a pier. This is a most delightful beach at low water, and a favourite spot for artists and also for children; but here again the visit should be paid, if possible, at low-water spring tides. Returning to the Boscastle Road, a descent of ½m. brings us to the Rocky Valley. A gate to the left leads down to a mill known as Creswick's Mill, through a lane in which the botanist will find the rare Cornish moneywort (*Sibthorpia Europœa*). On either hand the cliffs rise suddenly in such strange forms, and so covered with closely-clinging ivy, that it is almost impossible to believe but that they are groups of ruined castles. A lovely little stream tumbles down the valley, and empties itself into the sea; but those who would follow its course must be prepared for getting wet through. The return should be by the main road.

d. The road leads through Bossinney and down to Longbridge, which spans the stream that runs down Rocky Valley. It is almost worth while, before crossing the bridge, to turn up a lane to the right, and pass a mill, 100 yards above, which is one of the prettiest little cascades in Cornwall; but the visitor must be prepared

---

* This part has disappeared.

K

for a very rough scramble and for wet feet. ¼m. further up the hill is Trethevy Farm Place, where are some remains of old ecclesiastical buildings, and where the key and a guide may be procured for St. Nectan's or Nighton's Kieve*—a beautiful waterfall, well worth a visit. Carriages may be driven within a very short distance, by an upland road of 1m. from the farm; but the pedestrian would do well to descend into the valley and follow the path, half hidden by ferns and trees, along the brawling stream, to this lovely spot, admired and favoured of artists. On the summit of the fall, or rather falls, which are 40 or 50 feet high, are remains of a cottage, where two old ladies lived a mysterious and secluded life, and where they died—not altogether dissimilar in their history from the more celebrated "Ladies of Llangollen." It has been suggested that the cottage was formerly the site of a hermit's cell. This little excursion should on no account be omitted.

Regaining the Boscastle road at Trethevy, a walk of 1m. brings the traveller to *Trevalga* (= the walled place near the water), a hamlet of little interest save for its church, which was restored in 1874. The north chapel is the most interesting part; notice also the Norman font, and a hagioscope; and in the churchyard a rudely-sculptured cross. If some slight remains of a British village should prove an attraction, the tourist will find them (with some difficulty) at Penpethick, in the south part of the parish, in a field called Higher Marsh.

Before leaving Tintagel, the interesting old stone cross, perhaps as early as the 9th century, now set up in the little garden in front of the Wharncliffe Arms, should be noticed. It is of the Greek type, and is inscribed in Romano-Gothic characters—" Ælnat + fecit hanc crucem pro anima sua ;" on the other side are the names of the four Evangelists. The dressed stones which form part of the small heap surrounding it, are believed to be partly from the old town-hall which formerly stood at the upper end of the village, and partly from the remains of a priest's cell which once existed nearly opposite to the inn.

Leaving *Tintagel*, a road of about 3m. leads N.E.

---

* Kieve = basin; the word is still used in Cornwall to denote a large tub for water.

to *Boscastle*, the only object of interest passed on the way being *Forrabury* Church, with its still "silent tower" (the subject of one of Mr. Hawker's lovely poems*), and its old way-side cross inscribed on one side with the Greek and on the other with the Latin form of the symbol. The church, which contained some early work, has been restored, and some of its more interesting features have disappeared.

BOSCASTLE or Botreaux Castle, Castel Boterel,† &c., takes its name from the "castle," a circular, grass-grown mound, of which only the slightest traces now remain, situated at the point in Dun Street, called "Jordan" (?=the upper fort), where the two Boscastle valleys meet, overlooked by surrounding hills. It is a small, ancient village, on the slope of a steep hill;—the new road further west winding by a more gentle descent towards the bottom of the valley. There is an unusually good inn, the 'Wellington;' and lodgings are also attainable. The harbour is a remarkable instance of the triumph of human skill and perseverance, and the sight of a vessel's entering it,—especially if there is the least sea on—is one which should on no account be missed. The tortuous entrance—the warping-posts along the edges of the cliffs, and the huge cables laid ready for any emergency, will suggest to the tourist the character of the operation: Boscastle is one of the several examples of the difficulties of establishing a port on this part of the coast. The pier is of remote origin; indeed, it is said to have been rebuilt twice before 1584; and its decay at one period was an occasion of sore distress to the poor townsfolk, to whom its existence was a matter of great importance. There are several pleasant rambles in the neighbourhood of Boscastle, especially along its magnificent, breezy

* The story runs that on the approach to Boscastle of a ship which contained a peal of bells for the church, the pilot "thanked God" for a prosperous voyage, but the captain urged that the ship and crew ought to be thanked first; whereupon a great storm arose, which sank the vessel, cargo, and all the crew, except the pilot.

† The Boterels held lands in Cornwall at least as early as temp. Henry I. They appear to have been of Norman origin, but were virtually at last a Cornish family by long settlement. The late Marquis of Hastings was Baron Botreaux. Leland says that in his time the manor place was "of smaul reputation, far onworthe the name of a castel."

cliffs to the N.E. —towards *Pentargan* Waterfall (1m.),
150 feet high; near which, and at other parts of this
coast, are caverns known as seal-holes, which may be
visited during exceptionally fine weather, and where seals
are sometimes to be found "at home." The "blow holes,"
of which there are two good examples near the mouth of
the harbour, should also be looked out for; they are best
seen about one hour before low water. Nor will the
strange rock at Pelly Point—the harbour's mouth—
escape notice; it bears a striking resemblance to
Napoleon's head surmounted by the familiar cocked hat.
The appearance of Lundy Island, generally visible from
this part of the coast, from which it is distant about
37m., has given rise to the following weather proverb:

> " When Lundy is high it will be dry,
> When Lundy is plain it will be rain,
> When Lundy is low it will be snow."

But perhaps the most attractive ramble of all from
Boscastle is to *Minster* Church, 1m. S.E. of the inn: the
church key is kept by a person at Boscastle. The pedestrian may take the path up the wooded valley, and return
through the village; or go *vice versâ*. The site is seques-
tered, and fine old trees grow round the quiet churchyard
in the hollow. The church is situated on the site of an
alien Priory of Anjou, and was founded by one of the
Botreaux family. It was enlarged or rebuilt in the 16th
century; and was "restored" * about seven years ago. It
is mostly of the third Pointed period, but the east end and
the north-east angle are Early English. Some of the old
carved stones are to be found in unexpected parts of the
wall; e. g. the pair of scissors or shears at the north-west
angle of the tower. The only monument of special
interest is one to the Cotton family (middle of 17th
century), with its quaint conceit referring to the surviving
eight children, three sons and five daughters:

> " 3 Diatrite, 5 Diapente = 8 Diapason.
>
> In perfect concord may they still agree,
> Whose very numbers teach them harmony."

---

* During the restoration some of the old carved woodwork
was sold to private persons. If we mistake not, we recently saw
some of it in a shed at Trethevy Farm.

For those who are equal to a long, rough walk of 18m. along the cliffs, a great treat is in store if they resolve to *walk* from *Boscastle* to *Bude*. The road passes by a very pretty little cove, called Crackington Haven (6m.); thence (2m.) by the uninteresting *St. Gennys* Church, in which Captain Braddon, a distinguished Parliamentarian officer, was buried in 1694, to *Dazard Point* (= the high point), 550 feet above the sea. The carriage road is about the same length, passing near *Poundstock*.

BUDE (= ? a haven) is a favourite and growing watering-place: a local guide-book enumerates 70 lodging houses — besides the two inns, the 'Falcon' and the 'Bude.' The air is remarkably bracing, and the cliffs of contorted carbonaceous strata, fine; but they are crumbling away, and climbers should be very cautious. A railway is in course of construction from Oakhampton to *Holsworthy* (10m. from Bude). There is also a coach to Barnstaple (36m.) and another (20m.) to *Launceston*. The *church* was built about forty years ago. The *breakwater*, 900 feet long, serves as an esplanade for visitors, and affords some shelter for vessels up to 300 tons. A canal, 20m. long, with a branch to *Holsworthy*, connects *Bude* with *Launceston*, and is mainly used for carrying sand, for agricultural purposes, inland.* Bude is a terrible place for wrecks; and the boating and bathing are both dangerous. Here lived Goldsworthy Gurney, the inventor of the Bude light.

An up-hill excursion over rough roads may be made from *Bude* to *Morwenstow*, through *Stratton* and *Kilkhampton*; returning to Bude through *Stow*; the distances being approximately as follows, viz. *Bude* to *Stratton*, 2m.; *Stratton* to *Kilkhampton*, 3½m.; *Kilkhampton* to *Morwenstow*, 4m.; and *Morwenstow* back to *Bude* through *Stow*, 7m.; total about 17m.

STRATTON, whose name suggests a Roman origin, is a small and poor, but ancient market-town, "chiefly noted" (as an old writer says) "for gardens and garlick." The *church* is Perpendicular, and has been lately restored; it contains some brasses to the Arundel family, and has a fine tower. The register records the death

---

* 1½m. S.E. from Stratton on this canal is an inclined plane, worked on a curious principle, and altogether an ingenious piece of water engineering.

of Elizabeth Cornish in 1691, in her 114th year. On *Stamford Hill*, about ½m. N.W. of Stratton, was fought a great battle in 1643, during the Civil Wars, to which reference has already been made in the Section on *History*, and which resulted in a Royalist victory. Slight traces of one of the Parliamentarian earthworks are still to be seen on the summit; but the monument which was erected in 1713 by George Grenville, Lord Lansdowne (the last lineal descendant of the hero of the fight—Sir Bevil Grenville), has been taken down; the inscription is still preserved at the Tree Inn, at Stratton. The road now leads N.E. through *Barnacot* and *Hawston* to

KILKHAMPTON (= ? the Church Town). The church is interesting, especially that part of the Norman work visible at the south porch; but it is mainly Perpendicular, and was restored in 1860. Here, in a chapel south of the chancel, is the monument of the above-mentioned Sir Bevil Grenville, a worthy representative of another fine old Norman-Cornish family, who was slain in battle at Lansdowne, near Bath, on 5th July, 1643, shortly after the victory of Stamford Hill. Hervey—whose ' Meditations among the Tombs ' was a popular, though somewhat lugubrious volume, during the last century—was curate at Bideford whilst he composed that work, the idea of which occurred to him whilst visiting *Kilkhampton* Church and churchyard. It is reported that he received 700*l.* for the copyright of the first part, and that he devoted the money to charitable purposes. The road now passes N.W. through *Rats' Island* and *Woodford* (the tourist will notice in this district how the old *Cornish* names are disappearing), until we arrive at the northernmost parish of Cornwall,

MORWENSTOW (= the place of St. Morwenna). Here, besides the church, the only object of interest is the fine cliff scenery—especially *Hennacliff* (= the ravens' crag), a sheer precipice, 450 feet high, ¾m. N.W. of the church. The *church* is dedicated to St. Morwenna —whose well is still to be seen on the cliffs—and is chiefly Norman, the south porch here also being good. The carved bench-ends and screen are, of course, much later—indeed, some of the work is so recent as 1595 and 1664—but the font seems to be the original one. There are some monuments in the church to members of extinct and long-forgotten Cornish families; and in the churchyard, to more than one shipwrecked crew. *Morwenstow* is chiefly known from its eccentric poetic vicar, the late Rev. R. S. Hawker, whose secession to the Roman Catholic Church was recently a subject of much painful interest.

The more direct road from Morwenstow back to Bude (about 7m.) passes, half way, one interesting spot, near Coombe, namely, *Stow*; the site of the old mansion of the Grenvilles. No remains are now to be seen; but here lived the "father of his county,"—who called nearly every Cornish gentleman "cousin," and whose house was a rendezvous for the gentle youth, where they obtained sage counsel in war, and in the humanities.

The road from Bude to Launceston (20m.) calls for no special remark, except that, when approaching Launceston, the traveller passes for about 3m. across an outlying strip of Devon. The termination of the route, however, compensates for its dulness.

LAUNCESTON (= ? the Church of St. Stephen, or the Church Castle Town, or, if we try to interpret its old Celtic name, *Dunheved* * = the long, swelling hill) presents from most sides a striking appearance, but from none so fine a view as from the suburb of St. Stephens (whose Early English church, with a Perpendicular tower, was the mother church of Launceston before the present castle and town were built). It is now a little hamlet to the north of the town, through which the Bude coach passes.

The *Castle* forms the most prominent object of the landscape—Castle Terrible, as it has well been called. Ivy-covered, from the summit of a lofty, conical hill, the keep still frowns on the peaceful valleys at its foot, and still seems to defy the attempts of any invader who should presume to attack it or the dwellings of the quiet citizens sheltering under its walls. When it is added that Leland describes it as "the strongest though not the biggest that ever I saw in any ancient worke in Englande," the writer feels that he is justified in the promise given at p. 44, to provide a fit termination to a tour through Cornwall. Of the town walls, few remains are now to be seen; but the south gate, much

* A hill near Shaftesbury bears a somewhat similar name.

modernized and disfigured, still stands, and should be
seen. It reminds one of a similar work at Dinan, and
of another at Bergen. The *Castle* has been well described by Mr. S. R. Pattison, in the R.I.C.J., in 1851.
The site has probably, from its commanding position,
been occupied in succession by Roman, Saxon, and
Dane; but most of what remains is very late Norman.
The ground plan is an irregular parallelogram, 500
feet × 400 feet, with the keep on a high mound at the
south-east corner. The principal entrance is at the old
west gate-house, a fine, bold structure of two storeys,
with its portcullis groove, which has now, however,
lost all its details. A few steps within, on the right,
is a lodge gate (here get the key of the keep), through
which admission to the prettily laid-out gardens which
surround the keep is obtained. The grounds were
laid out at the cost of Constable His Grace the Duke
of Northumberland. The open space on the left, once
the base court, but from which all buildings have now
disappeared, was within living memory the place for
executing criminals; it is now used for the pleasanter
purpose of a playground by the rising generation of
Launceston. At its eastern side is the picturesque east
gate, where George Fox, the Quaker, was imprisoned for
"disturbing the public peace," in 1656, by distributing
tracts at St. Ives; the little chamber is still to be seen,
and is known as Doomsdale.* To describe the curious
keep, with its two concentric walls—a most singular
structure, the ascent to which is by a steep flight of
steps, near the foot of which is a postern leading to the
town—would occupy more space than remains at our
command; but it is well worthy of examination, and
should be compared with the sister works of *Restormel*
and *Trematon*, as well as with portions of *Tintagel*.†
The old fire-place in the interior is still in fair preserva-
tion, and is well seen on the way up by a winding stair-
case to the summit, the view from which is very fine.

* Mr. Pattison observes that here Agnes Prest was burnt by
Queen Mary "for denying Popish tenets"; here, under Queen
Elizabeth, Cuthbert Mayne "was hanged for upholding them";
and here, under Cromwell, a similar doom fell upon certain
worthy "citizens of London and Bristol for being Quakers."

† The destroyed castles of *Truro* and *Liskeard* were, no doubt,
somewhat similar to this part of *Launceston*.

At the south-west angle of the castle enclosure is the site of the Witches' or Giants' Tower, deriving the former name from its having been the place where "witches" were once burnt, and the latter from some human remains of gigantic size which were discovered when the new road here was formed in 1834. Launceston Castle was probably commenced by Earl Moreton, soon after the Conquest: at his decease it became an appanage of the Crown, but was rarely occupied, so that, on its annexation to the Duchy in 1337, it was already decaying; and of its park, "a league in circuit, containing fifteen deer," only the name now remains. In 1650 it was much out of repair; the hall and chapel had been levelled to the ground, and no part of the castle was habitable save the gateway, where the Constable lodged. During the Civil Wars the castle had a chequered history. First, Sir Richard Buller held it for the Parliament, but fled on the approach of the Royalists; who in their turn held it against the Parliamentarians. In August, 1644, however, they surrendered it to Essex;—on the capitulation of his army it fell again into the hands of the Royalists; was occupied by Prince Charles in 1645; and was ultimately surrendered to Fairfax on the final defeat of the Royal cause. The assizes were held within the walls of the castle till the time of Richard, King of the Romans, who transferred them to Lostwithiel; but they were soon restored to Launceston. In 1716 the summer assizes were removed to Bodmin, and in 1838 the winter assizes followed. The county gaol was here until 1780, when it also was removed to Bodmin, but the gaol establishment was not entirely broken up till 1829.

The *Church*, dedicated to St. Mary Magdalene (a recumbent figure of whom may be seen in a recess of the external wall of the eastern end), is one of the handsomest in Cornwall, though it possesses no very ancient portions. It is almost entirely of granite, richly sculptured in panels, with a few figures, including St. George and St. Martin; there is also a long Latin invocation to the Virgin, which commences at the priests' door and goes round the church. The church is said to have been built before 1524, with stones originally designed for a mansion by Sir Henry Trecarrel, of Trecarrel, 6m. S. of Launceston (an old Cornish house well worth an excursion). The south porch resembles that of Truro, and bears the

date 1511. The interior of the church presents nothing
of special interest, except, perhaps, the font (till recently
used as a trough), the pulpit, and the tomb of Sir Hugh
Pyper (1687), a Royalist soldier, who once represented
Launceston in Parliament. The space between the old
tower and the church, occupied since 1810 as a council
room by the Corporation, was formerly the site of two
ancient houses.

There was a Priory in the western suburb of Launceston, founded temp. Henry I.; but few, if any, remains
of it exist, though it was once the wealthiest in Cornwall. The handsome Norman doorway of the White Hart
Inn came from the Priory.

L'ENVOI.

Such are the attractions of *Launceston*—a place which
seems no unfitting point of departure from venerable
Cornwall. Of the attractions of Devon, whose borders,
defined by the Tamar, lie about 2m. east of Launceston
by the railway line, other writers will treat. I will only
add that I would strongly recommend that the return
route to London should be by the rail from Lidford,
which passes by the ancient town and abbey of Tavistock—for the most part along the wooded valley of the
river Tavy on the one hand, and the heathery, granite
moors of Dartmoor on the other—till the tourist reaches
Plymouth, where we assumed the post of mentor, and
where we now bid him—in the good *old* sense of the
words—Good-bye!

INDEX.

GUIDE BOOKS FOR ENGLISH TOURISTS,

PUBLISHED BY

EDWARD STANFORD, 55, Charing Cross, S.W.

ENGLISH LAKES. — JENKINSON'S PRACTICAL GUIDE TO THE ENGLISH LAKE DISTRICTS. Containing full Information and Instructions respecting Walks, Drives, Boating, Ascents, Excursions, &c., with Charges for Conveyances, Ponies, and Guides; Heights of Mountains, Lakes, Tarns, and Passes; Local Names; Meteorology, Geology, and Botany. Fifth Edition, with Nine Maps and Three Panoramic Views, fcap. 8vo, cloth, 6s.

** The SECTIONS separately:—KESWICK—WINDERMERE and LANGDALE—CONISTON, BUTTERMERE and WASTWATER—GRASMERE and ULLSWATER. With Maps, 1s. 6d. each.

Also, A SMALLER PRACTICAL GUIDE to the English Lakes, by the same Author. With Maps, 1s. 6d.

ISLE OF MAN.—JENKINSON'S PRACTICAL GUIDE TO THE ISLE OF MAN. With Chapters on Local Names, Mineralogy, Civil History, Ecclesiastical History, Geology, Botany, Zoology, Agriculture, Commerce, and Sea Trout-fishing. Fcap. 8vo, with Map, cloth, 5s.

Also, A SMALLER PRACTICAL GUIDE to the Isle of Man, by the same Author. With Map, 2s.

CARLISLE, ROMAN WALL, &c. — JENKINSON'S PRACTICAL GUIDE TO CARLISLE, GILSLAND, the ROMAN WALL, and NEIGHBOURHOOD. With Chapters on Local Names, Geology, Mineralogy, Botany, Butterflies, and Birds. Fcap. 8vo, cloth, with Map, 5s.

Also, A SMALLER PRACTICAL GUIDE to Carlisle, &c., by the same Author. With Map, 2s.

ISLE OF WIGHT. — JENKINSON'S PRACTICAL GUIDE TO THE ISLE OF WIGHT. With Chapters on the Local Names, the History, Geology, Botany, Quadrupeds, Reptiles, Fresh-water Fishes, Birds, and Butterflies; the Fortifications, Agriculture, Commerce, and Fisheries of the Island. Fcap. 8vo, cloth, with Frontispiece and Six Maps, 5s.

Also, A SMALLER PRACTICAL GUIDE to the Isle of Wight, by the same Author. With Map, 2s.

LONDON GUIDE.—What and How to See, with Times, Prices, Routes, Fares, &c., arranged alphabetically and in Tables for ready reference. Crown 8vo, with Map, 3s. 6d.

ROUND ABOUT LONDON.—TOURIST'S GUIDE TO THE COUNTRY WITHIN A CIRCLE OF TWELVE MILES ROUND ABOUT LONDON. Comprising a List of the Parishes, Towns, Villages, Hamlets, Parks, Seats, Churches, Livings, Monuments, and Eminent Inhabitants. With Historical, Archæological, Architectural, and Picturesque Notes, suitable for the Tourist, Antiquarian, and Artist. Compiled from the best ancient and modern authorities and from actual observation. To which is added a Series of Specimens of Walking Excursions, limited to Six Miles, and Visits to Hatfield, Knole, St. Albans, and Windsor, with a copious Index. By A FELLOW OF THE SOCIETY OF ANTIQUARIES. Fcap. 8vo, cloth, with Map, 2s.

LONDON : EDWARD STANFORD, 55, CHARING CROSS, S.W.

YORKSHIRE.—TOURIST'S GUIDE TO THE EAST
AND NORTH RIDINGS OF YORKSHIRE. Containing full Information
concerning all its favourite Places of Resort, both on the Coast and Inland.
By G. PHILLIPS BEVAN, F.G.S. With Map, and Plan of York Minster.
Fcap. 8vo, cloth, 2s.

YORKSHIRE.—TOURIST'S GUIDE TO THE WEST
RIDING OF YORKSHIRE. Containing full information concerning all
its principal Places of Resort and Interest. By G. PHILLIPS BEVAN, F.G.S.
Fcap. 8vo, cloth, with Maps, 2s.

DERBY.—TOURIST'S GUIDE TO THE COUNTY OF
DERBY. With full Information relative to the principal Places and
Objects of Interest therein. By J. C. COX, author of 'Notes on the
Churches of Derbyshire.' With Map. Fcap. 8vo, cloth, 2s.

KENT.—TOURIST'S GUIDE TO THE COUNTY OF
KENT. Containing full Information concerning all its favourite Places of
Resort, both on the Coast and Inland, with General Description of the
County, and Instructions respecting Excursions by Railway, Steamboat,
and Road. By G. PHILLIPS BEVAN, F.G.S. Fcap. 8vo, cloth, with Map,
and Plans of Canterbury and Rochester Cathedrals, 2s.

SUSSEX.—TOURIST'S GUIDE TO THE COUNTY OF
SUSSEX. Containing full Information concerning all its favourite Places
of Resort, both on the Coast and Inland. By G. F. CHAMBERS, F.R.A.S.,
Barrister-at-Law; author of 'A Handbook for Eastbourne,' &c. Fcap.
8vo, with Map, and Plan of Chichester Cathedral, cloth, 2s.

DEVON.—TOURIST'S GUIDE TO SOUTH DEVON:
Rail, Road, River, Coast, and Moor. By R. N. WORTH, F.G.S., &c.; author
of 'History of Plymouth,' 'The Progress of Mining Skill in the West of
England,' &c. With Map, and Plan of Exeter Cathedral. Fcap. 8vo,
cloth, 2s.

CORNWALL.—TOURIST'S GUIDE TO CORNWALL
AND THE SCILLY ISLES. Containing Information concerning all
the principal Places and Objects of Interest in the County. By WALTER
H. TREGELLAS, Chief Draughtsman, War Office. With Map. Fcap. 8vo,
cloth, 2s.

EASTBOURNE.—HANDBOOK FOR EASTBOURNE,
SEAFORD, AND THE NEIGHBOURHOOD. By G. F. CHAMBERS,
F.R.A.S., Barrister-at-Law. Eighth Edition, crown 8vo, 1s.; with Map,
1s. 4d.; in cloth, with Maps, 2s.

WEYMOUTH.—GUIDE TO THE GEOLOGY OF
WEYMOUTH AND THE ISLAND OF PORTLAND; containing a
Geological Map of the District, Geological Sections, Coast Views, Figures
of the characteristic Fossils, and other Illustrations; with numerous Notes
on the Botany and Zoology of the Coast and Neighbourhood. By ROBERT
DAMON. Fcap. 8vo, cloth, 5s.
A Supplement to the above, consisting of Nine Lithographic Plates of
Fossils, drawn by BONE. 2s. 6d.

CHANNEL ISLANDS.—GUIDE TO JERSEY AND
GUERNSEY; with Notes on their History, Geology, Climate, Agriculture, Laws, &c. By F. F. DALLY. Third Edition, with Maps, fcap. 8vo,
cloth, 3s. 6d.

LONDON: EDWARD STANFORD, 55, CHARING CROSS, S.W.

CPSIA information can be obtained
at www.ICGtesting.com
Printed in the USA
BVHW03*1548230818
525434BV00003B/8/P

9 781165 176618